Paul Peacock has been making sausages at home for twenty or more years. He regularly teaches sausage-making courses at conferences and shows around the UK, and has filmed an entire series of sausage-making recipes for daytime television. Along with his wife Diana, Paul believes the best food you will ever eat is produced in your own kitchen, and the recipes in this book have stood the test of time, family and the general public. Paul has written more than thirty books on self-sufficiency, and can be found on radio stations around the UK including being a regular contributor to BBC Radio 4's *Gardeners' Question Time*. He also writes a weekly column for the *Daily Mirror* as Mr Digwell.

Also by Paul Peacock

Making Your Own Cheese
Make Your Own Beer and Cider
Chickens, Ducks and Bees
The Urban Hen
Grandma's Ways for Modern Days
Patio Produce

HOW TO MAKE
YOUR OWN
SAUSAGES

Paul Peacock

ROBINSON

ROBINSON

First published in Great Britain in 2015 by Robinson

Text copyright © Paul Peacock, 2015

The moral right of the author has been asserted.

A CIP catalogue record for this book is available from the British Library.

ISBN: 978-1-84528-591-3 (paperback)
ISBN: 978-1-84528-593-7 (ebook)

The material contained in this book is set out for general guidance and does not
deal with any particular and personal circumstances. Laws and regulations are
complex and liable to change, and readers should check the current position with
relevant authorities before making individual arrangements and where necessary
take appropriate advice.

Typeset in Great Britain by Ian Hughes, Mousemat Design Limited
Printed and bound by CPI Group (UK) Ltd, Croydon, CR0 4YY

Robinson
is an imprint of
Constable & Robinson Ltd
100 Victoria Embankment
London EC4Y 0DY

An Hachette UK Company
www.hachette.co.uk

www.constablerobinson.com

Contents

Acknowledgements

Thanks to Jane Donovan for editing this book so manfully. To Darren Wright for reading through the manuscript and Joshua, Joel and Rebecca Peacock for stuffing their faces with sausages over the years.

Thanks also to the manufacturers of sausage skins without whom my marriage would not have been saved!

Introduction

Sausages and their history

When we think of warfare in these modern times we might picture a fast jet or a battleship, a nuclear weapon or sarin gas. Some of us might remember the Spitfire or the Chieftain tank. Going back into pre-history, warfare was more desperate. It consisted of brave men, sometimes on horseback, often on foot, prepared to rip you open with a piece of sharp metal and then stand their ground. The sausage was a weapon of mass destruction in as much as it enabled lots of such warriors to travel long distances.

Without the sausage, none of the great civilisations of the Old Testament would have existed in the same way. There would be no Egypt for Joseph to take his family into, no Nebuchadnezzar to rule the whole of the known world.

The sausage, first and foremost, is a way of preserving meat and other food, and this not only fed us in times of feast and famine, but guaranteed people, armies and sailors mostly the ability to travel great distances and not run out of food. The salting of sausages – the very word sausage means 'salted' – also allowed the movement of food over great distances in a convenient form more or less impervious to insects. Anyone who has tried to cure a ham will know that salt alone is not enough to keep the meat safe. Many a piece of pork has been ruined by the action of insects laying their eggs in the meat, but a sausage, in an intestine skin, is more or less safe from the ovipositors of spoiling creatures.

In the Roman army, generals would eat fowl and other animals taken fresh from the lands they happened to find themselves in. Centurions would eat salted beef and lamb, but ordinary foot soldiers, working off their slavery by enslaving others, would eat strangely fermented fish soup and Lucanian sausage (a recipe for this can be found later on page 120). These were shipped from

Italy, Spain and Turkey to the whole of the Roman world, as far as Hadrian's Wall. Consequently any list of 'What the Romans did for us' should include the sausage, as well as enslavement, the mass destruction of civilisations and the peptic ulcer.

Interestingly, Scotland doesn't have quite the tradition of sausages as we know them in the rest of the UK, nor does Ireland, but local sausages, particularly pork sausages in England and Wales, have long been associated with flavours that can be grown locally, such as sage or apple, and a particular breed of pig. The reason why we have so many different types of sausage in England is because in the Napoleonic Wars individual counties and individual families provided food for their regiments so we have a Lincolnshire sausage that was sent for the Lincolnshires, increasingly by canal barge to the nearest sea port, allowing a fast and constant food supply, unlike the French, whose supplies took weeks longer to arrive at the battle lines. It was the canal system and sausages that beat Napoleon. Later, parcels of sausages from various counties sent to the troops in France and Belgium during World War I were simply named Lincolnshire or Derby. These sausages were then directed to the regiments originating from those localities.

The other function performed by sausages was to make something we would naturally recoil from eating into something completely wonderful. Fat sausages in France, that is big fat, juicy sausages made from fat, became *boudin blanc*, something not that popular in the UK, but wonderful nonetheless. Blood sausages became *boudin noir* or black pudding. Particularly treasured in Lancashire and parts of Yorkshire, home-kept pigs were expensive meat and all the poor had left to eat once the great monasteries had taken their share of the cuts for the brothers who owned the land the pig peasants farmed, were oats grown locally (the North of England is generally not wheat country) and blood from the slaughtered pig. But cooked in a sausage, black pudding becomes one of the most marvellous delicacies.

Similarly, haggis is a combination of lights or pluck, oatmeal and herbs. Lights or pluck are the heart, lungs and windpipe of an animal, and to sit down to a meal of such on a plate would put all but the most carnivorous of us off eating for a week or more. However, ground with oats and stuffed into a stomach, boiled or baked, they become one of our culinary wonders. Look out for our recipe for haggis mash (page 164) – you'll never have a shepherd's pie any other way in future.

Trading of sausages

The keeping properties of sausage led to their trade but, the actual origin of sausage making is not clear. In order to make sausage you need salt, meat, fresh running water and the ability to empty and clean the guts of an animal. In a way, piety played its part, too, in the development of the sausage. Almost every civilisation has a religious abhorrence of waste at its core, and finding something useful to do with intestines reflects this. The gut is a remarkable piece of technology. It makes strong rope, the very best musical instruments, excellent containers for food and was probably important in the development of cheese. (Cheese-making became the main use for young male calves for rennet, itself made by drying and powdering the stomach of young cattle. Males generally were of little use around the farm and were quickly dispatched for food.) The gut also makes excellent weapons, including the sling shot, bow strings and, in more modern times, Zeppelins!

Trade in sausages is recorded first in Greece, probably because they had a reliable, long-lasting system of writing and were able to record their transactions rather than because they were first to trade sausages. There are plenty of examples of sausages being traded around the world, from earlier times. Parys Mountain, Anglesey, and the Great Orme in Llandudno in the Bronze and Iron Ages were centres of copper mining visited from all parts of the ancient world, and trade in food was a part of this activity. For some roundhouse dwellers, inland of the Welsh coast, highly spiced sausage was a common food long before a full Welsh breakfast was even conceived of.

Early sausages were air-dried, probably from the Mediterranean, where the climate was sufficiently dry for long enough to allow enough water to be removed from the sausage to enhance the keeping properties of salt. It was the Romans who brought in the smoking of sausages, which apart from providing enhanced flavour also had extra keeping qualities, and with this the science of dried sausages was almost complete. Sausages were made safe to eat even months after they were prepared in four separate systems. We will look at this in future chapters in more detail, but it is worth noting the skill of the Roman sausage makers.

Salting preserves in two ways. First of all it is directly poisonous to spoiling bacteria and fungi, and therefore kills them. This process is enhanced by some of the spices added to sausages. Salt also draws water from the meat and anything growing in it by osmosis. This is such a violent effect that the removal of water from bacteria and fungi by salt often ruptures and therefore kills the organism. Air-drying also reduces the amount of water in the sausage, increasing the osmotic effect and making it a barren and arid place for spoiling microbes to live.

Fermentation releases acids into the meat, so the use of a fermenting microbe in the sausage, for products like chorizo, makes it more difficult for microbes to live and grow in the meat. Finally, smoking sausages not only produces volatile chemicals that kill spoiling microbes, but the particles of smoke also make it less likely for anything that lands on the sausage to gain a foothold and grow into it.

The Lucanian sausage, coming from a region in Southern Italy, travelled the world with the armies of Rome, but as legions found themselves at the loneliest extremes of the Empire, it became increasingly difficult to follow the Lucanian recipe in climates too damp to allow sufficient air drying. As you travel north from the Mediterranean, the climate becomes more and more humid. Trying to dry out an air-dried sausage that typically loses 30 per cent of its weight by evaporation is not so easy. From Biblical times until the Middle Ages there is little in the way of Northern European air-dried sausage manufacture, though there are many records for Eastern Europe, Turkey and Bulgaria – countries with dry climates in the summer. However, it is reasonable to speculate that the development of what can be called 'wet sausages', including the British banger, is a result of multiple technologies and closely linked to that other great foodstuff we have in the West – hamburgers!

When I was a boy you would find many hamburger salesmen who would also sell hot dog sausages, cooked in boiling water, served on a long bun with onions and mustard. It is perhaps fitting that the hot dog and the hamburger should be sold together.

Genghis Khan in the twelfth century formed the largest empire that has ever been seen in history. It took in most of Asia, stretched into Europe and as far north as Russia. His mounted soldiers were given their daily allocation of meat, which would be rubbed with salt and spices and placed under their saddles to be tenderised before being eaten raw. When the Tartars, a European name for the Mongolian hordes, entered Moscow, the inhabitants loved the raw meat and it became very popular. Steak Tartare (raw mince, sometimes spiced, sometimes with a raw egg on the top) is the modern remnant of this diet.

As the Tartars retreated homeward, local skirmishes and trade in Eastern Europe took this food to Germany, where it was adored and became known as 'meat in the Hamburg fashion'. Of course, we know the cooked version as hamburgers. However, it is a small step to put this meat into skins instead of eating it as a patty and the good old banger was born.

Wet sausages have shorter keeping properties than air-dried ones. Uncooked, they last about a week and, consequently, don't travel well. Those of the view that sausages are a rural invention miss the mark when it comes to wet sausages since they need to be made and sold reasonably quickly and therefore tend to be from a particular locality, like a large village, or a small town.

The beginning of the twelfth century saw the development of gunpowder and with the mass production of saltpetre (some spell it 'saltpeter') in Syria, it became a common chemical throughout Europe. Indeed, in the UK, the Saltpetre men could come and tear down your toilet to extract the salts left behind by your kidneys! However, its use in sausage and meat preservation was still some way off.

The possible link between incorrectly prepared sausages and illness goes far back. In the tenth century the Byzantine Pope Leo VI banned the production of blood sausages, possibly partly from a misunderstanding about the scriptures, but also most likely following numerous deaths after consumption.

Generally speaking, saltpetre became a common additive to cured meat products and is now compulsory, though in much smaller quantities than formerly. Poisoning by sausage was fairly common in Germany, and around the year 1817, the recorder and medical officer Justinus Kerner called the disease botulism because of the link with sausage (*botulus* means sausage in Latin). A celebrated poisoning at a funeral in Belgium in 1735 led to the isolation of the pathogen, *Clostridium botulinum*. It is the addition of saltpetre that specifically kills this bacterium, making sausages much safer. Any sausage for sale, or to be given to anyone else to eat, now has to contain saltpetre, but in tightly controlled quantities. It is compulsory worldwide if you plan to sell your cured products or if you are going to get other people (including members of your own family) to eat what you have made.

Whereas the spread of sausages around the Old World was purely military at first, its transit to the New World, and thence back round the world again, was economically driven. The movement of the German people from Frankfurt, Bonn, Vienna and Hamburg from 1800 onwards, largely to avoid war or hunger (often both), had a great effect on the United States. For a while there was some debate about the possibility of the official language being German.

Back in Frankfurt, development of the rather long but thick sausages coincided with the rise in popularity of their favourite 'little-dogs' (dachshunds). The sausages became known as little-dogs, and when butchers moved to America they took their dogs and their sausages with them. The hot-dog has numerous origins, but people selling 'dogs' on street corners with sauerkraut and bread buns proved very popular. A number of historians suggest that the term hot-dog was coined at Yale University, where cooked sausages were sold to students from carts. Of course, the Wiener from Vienna and the Frankfurter continued as a sausage bought from butchers and were eventually shipped around the world with a new-found American commercial slant.

Although the sausage is currently enjoying a resurgence in popularity, the way we buy and eat it has changed in recent times. The word 'banger' comes from World War II and has associated the sausage with the stigma of exploding panfuls of water and fat, fairly tasteless and packed with salt. The sausages of the early twentieth century were emergency sausages, with not much in the way of meat, too much water and a lot of rusk or breadcrumbs. Consequently when cooked, they often exploded – a problem half-remedied by pricking the sausage, which actually just let all the flavour out!

British sausages took on a general decline since that time, but there have been greater problems associated with the growth of supermarkets. Selling sausages off the shelf, along with bacon and other meat products, has reduced the number of butchers on the high street. In North Manchester in the 1970s there were 50 butchers creating their own sausage from pork shoulder meat (study carried out for the *Middleton Guardian*). Thirty years later that number has dropped, certainly to less than three. This is a picture repeated around the UK. Sausages are bought wrapped in plastic, off the supermarket shelf. Mostly, it is the quality of the sausage that has suffered. There is little to choose between one packet of pink sausages and another, hence the consumer is not easily able to know which is a prime product. Once upon a time the shoppers only had to ask the butcher, who would usually regale them about the quality of his sausage.

On the other hand, supermarkets have brought a greater variety of sausages to the table. There was once, on the high street of many communities, a pork shop. They sold items like brawn, pressed ham, faggots, haggises and sausages, and sometimes what we called 'party sausage', incorrectly named chipolata by some. They would, from time to time, sell garlic sausage, but you would generally have to go to a delicatessen to get more exotic sausage. The supermarket, with its packaged sandwich meat and frozen foods, has resulted in the closure of such pork shops, but they are now full of sausages from around the world. Where once you could get salami only if you were lucky, and liver sausage came in an inedible plastic tube, you now have chorizo from Spain (indeed, you can get 300 different types from almost every village, some with mixed meats, some with various herbs, others with mushrooms or wild boar instead of pig meat), Polish kabano, kielbasa and umpteen different sausages from Eastern Europe, German sausages, Mexican sausages and, if you look carefully, a whole range of sausages from China and the Far East.

All these sausages are the result of the internationalisation of food, and in particular the growing popularity of pizza and the race for more and more different toppings. Sausage such as the fiery nduja from Mexico would never formerly have gone anywhere other than the locality in which it was made, but can now be found on the deli counters of supermarkets the world over, thanks to the efforts of Pizza Hut and Pizza Express.

The use of sausage as an ingredient rather than a food product in its own right has long accounted for at least 50 per cent of its use. The Toulouse sausage was specifically designed as an ingredient for cassoulet; using sausage more imaginatively, in soups and stews, on pizza, to top lasagna and numerous pasta dishes is bringing the sausage into a new field of culinary expertise. Moreover, sausages such as black pudding have found their way into some of the most illustrious restaurants in the world, often topped with exotic ingredients such as quail eggs or caviar, even chocolate.

There exists, though, a growing number of premium sausages. Made in the style of more ancient fashion when they were never thought to be mere bangers, they recreate the qualities that made them great – good meat, fine herbs, and just the right amount of seasoning. Butchers around the UK have found that people are prepared to pay a little extra for a better product, and the breakfast sausage is on its way up. But there is a long way to go for the humble sausage. This book is largely about making your own, and this brings you into a whole new world. There is a huge difference between a sausage that has the luxurious meat content at 45 per cent and a homemade version with a meat content of 70 per cent. Homemade sausages hark back to a time when they were always made by hand, always filled with the best ingredients and tasted so much better than any other foodstuff anywhere!

Suppliers

The following online retailers can sell you the equipment and specialist ingredients you need to start making your own sausages.

Ascott Smallholder supplies
www.ascott-dairy.co.uk
01626 880894

Designasausage
www.designasausage.com
01663 764208

Lakeland
www.lakeland.co.uk
01539 488100

SausageMaking
www.sausagemaking.org
0845 693 6915

Weschenfelder
www.weschenfelder.co.uk
01624 241395

Chapter 1

Why make your own sausages?

You do not need a lot of equipment to make sausages. In fact you don't even need skins as you can make skinless sausages and cover them in so many different ways as we will see with many of the recipes in this book. But eventually you will want to make linked, skinned sausages and consequently you will have some outlay, which is essentially a stuffer/grinder and some skins. Of course, you will get so much use from the stuffer/grinder beyond making sausages, it will pay for itself many times over inside six months. We generally make minced meat from all kinds of sources; offcuts and bits of bacon make great pâté. And we also use it to make corned beef and sandwich meat. With a special attachment, you can use it to make your own pasta too.

Then the cost of your sausages is such that you will have the very best for around a third of the price. It is impossible to beat the price of economy sausages from the supermarket, made by machine, with dubious meat, but it is possible to make your own versions of the most expensive luxury sausages for not much more than the price of the cheap ones. However, that is only if you are buying your meat. If you keep your own pigs you can make sausages for even less. Some abattoirs will make sausage for you, presenting you with various joints and a few bags of sausages to your specification. Butchers usually bone out a pork shoulder, as this has an ideal fat ratio for sausages and there are still some abattoirs that will bone out for you too. However, producing your own mince from a shoulder is not that difficult, and you then have the perfect basis for your own sausages.

Quality and flavour

You cannot compare your homemade sausage with a bought one. The quality and flavour is so much better, mostly because the meat content is much higher than in those bought from shops. But there are other factors too. Although they do need salt, and probably saltpetre too, homemade sausages can have the very best ingredients in them. For example, there is no need for colours, stabilisers or other preservatives. The spices you add are yours, as fresh as you like. And the meat you use is the best quality you can afford. Instead of eating the ground up face and other bits of a pig, you are eating the very best meat. Not that I have anything against pig's face … it is extremely tasty, but you get the idea.

Then again, when buying sausages from the supermarket – and let's face it, most of us do – you are paying the supermarket for all the chemicals needed to keep the product edible while it stays on the shelf, while it remains in cold storage, while it is transported around the country, and yes, even the world. To be honest, I am really glad supermarket sausages actually do have these chemicals in them and have all those systems to keep them good on the shelf and in refrigerated display otherwise they would literally be deadly. But I much prefer my own sausages, thank you very much!

Different varieties

The homemade sausage can reflect the traditional product. After all, someone first made a Lincolnshire sausage, or a polony (Bologna sausage) or a salami in a house, or perhaps, and most likely, a monastery. But the homemade sausage can go much further than that. Specific sausages we buy today became popular because people made them time and again in their homes. It is only in the last 150 years that this practice has become less popular. Your favourite sausage, the one you make week in, week out, might one day become a staple in years to come.

Our own sausage making for our family needs generally looks like this. First of all there is the basic sausage we make. We probably make between 2 and 5 kilos of these sausages in a batch and they last around six weeks, in separate bags, which are vacuum sealed. The approximate constitution is 75 per cent pork, 15 per cent breadcrumbs and the rest water, with around

1.5 per cent salt and a liberal amount of pepper. The meat for this batch of sausage varies too. We shop at the local food market, where you get some brilliant deals. Sometimes fresh pork mince is available, sometimes it is diced pork shoulder, and I grind it at home. Sometimes it's just a joint of meat that requires a little more work to get it ready for a sausage stuffer.

I always make sure the meat stays below 5°C (41°F), bringing it home with bags of ice cubes, and that way we make up our basic sausage ration. But then we make all kinds of sausage depending on what people like, and you can't always buy them. So, for example, I will make a batch of Chinese sweet chilli sauce sausages, and I am fairly sure I've never seen anything even close on sale in a supermarket. Essentially they are made by replacing the water content of the sausage with bottled sweet chilli sauce. It works a treat and people love them. The same goes for oyster sauce sausages.

I can make gluten-free sausages for my son's girlfriend, who cannot tolerate bread, and I also make really exotic sausages when I feel like showing off. For example, my beef and Stilton sausages are somewhat amazing, especially with some chives added to the mixture.

In this book you will find information on why southern Europe has dried sausages and northern Europe tends not to. I happen to live in one of the wettest valleys in Lancashire, and air drying without a posh cabinet is really difficult, but I like chorizo! So I have invented a version of a garlic chorizo that you simply cannot buy. It's hot even when it's eaten cold and wonderfully spicy too. Actually it is brilliant in a salad. But rather than air-drying it, this one is cooked, and once cooked, can be frozen for storage.

You can experiment

You will find one of the greatest joys of making your own sausages is to experiment with ideas, to find a sausage and then recreate it. For example, we have already mentioned nduja. Some people say this is an Italian sausage, but it has been developed in

Mexico too. It is a hot paste, placed in a skin and is often eaten by opening the skin and using the contents. I first came across it at Pizza Hut on a pizza called 'The Etna'. It has bits of nduja on the surface, and I was very impressed. Although rather too hot for my comfort, I decided to make my own version.

On the Web there are a number of recipes for nduja, some of them 30 per cent hot chillies. Too much for me! But I eventually settled on a sausage made from tomato, pimentón, chilli and finely ground beef. Hot, but not so hot that you can't eat it like salami, it is excellent on pizza and obviously, thousands will say, 'That's not nduja!' but who cares? They didn't make it.

You will find recipes for gourmet sausages in this book that I expect you to change. One of my favourites is venison with port. Now venison is a very lean meat with a rich flavour so you need to add fat. Instead of water I add a mixture of wine and port, which is cool by me because you can have a little sip while you are at it! Adding fat is almost always done by cutting pieces of pork back fat into small cubes. The same goes for pigeon and some other game, such as rabbit.

Get to know your butcher

You will have noticed that some of our sausages are made from meat purchased as cheaply as possible. Often we simply buy minced pork from the supermarket and make sausages with that, no grinding necessary. But this isn't always possible. You cannot go to the supermarket and get a piece of back fat, or a rabbit or pigeon – well, mostly you can't.

Whereas you wouldn't necessarily buy all your meat from a high-class butcher, you do need to build up a relationship with one, and that involves spending a little money from time to time. For example, when I moved into a new village I went to the butcher to buy some back fat but he didn't have any. He could get me some a week on Thursday, but not that day. A similar story repeated itself around the local area until I found someone able to sell me a piece of fat. He wrapped it, I took it home. When I opened it what I actually had was a piece of very old beef fat!

Finding a butcher who is sympathetic to your needs is important but these days it can be difficult. When you find a good butcher, he needs to be encouraged. I used to live in North Manchester, where there were 50 butchers. Now there are three and one sells only pre-frozen meat, another has cheap meat that is obtained ready-cut from a wholesalers and the final one was so expensive you couldn't continue to buy all your meat there, but at least he was a proper butcher, worthy of the name. From time to time I still visit him for back fat and other meat even though it is now an hour's drive away.

You can choose your own meat

It goes without saying that meat is an important part of the sausage, unless you are making a vegetarian sausage or even a seafood sausage (yes, they are possible). The cut of meat is up to you, obviously the meatier the better. For choice, pork shoulder is about right for general sausage making because on the whole it contains just 15–20 per cent fat, and we shall see later that fat is important in sausage making. Using pork shoulder there is not that much need to add extra fat unless the recipe specifically calls for it.

Most butchers order their pigs for mid-week and then bone out the shoulders mostly for sausage making in time for the weekend rush. You can combine pork cuts, though. For example, you might be able to only have leg (supermarkets often mince all their shoulder) so mix this with some belly.

You can use beef, or beef and pork. I try to use shin or chuck, the cheaper cuts.

You will make the best sausages for less cost

Some supermarket meat can be very old, around a month old, and is therefore more likely to spoil than fresher meat. Also, your meat might have been frozen at some time. Always ask if it can be frozen, as well as determining its age. Do not buy meat for sausage making that has already been frozen. When meat is frozen, many of the cells are broken by the ice and when this thaws the cell contents spill out onto the tissues. The juices are full of sugar and other nutrients and cause the development of spoiling bacteria, some of which can be harmful.

Better-quality meat will produce better sausages. Consequently, for everyday eating a balance between convenience, cost and quality is struck. Moreover, the amount of sausage you make is important. Usually the recipes in this book are for making a couple of kilos of sausages. However, if you make 10 kilos, this has implications on the sausage making process. For example, a slip up in the amount of salt has greater consequences if you only make a kilo than if you make 10 kilos. Equally, temperature control of a large quantity of meat is easier than a smaller amount.

Anyone can buy cheap sausages but making your own is more about making the very best sausages for the lowest price.

You can use different meats

Chicken is good in sausages, as is venison, lamb, goat, fish (yes, fish and more on that later), game including rabbit and pigeon, turkey and goose, and duck, which makes possibly the best Chinese spiced sausages there is.

You'll enjoy making your own sausages

I suppose, more than anything else, I make sausages because I enjoy it. If I make a batch of 5 kilos of sausage it takes me all afternoon. Maybe if I was in a job that paid average wages I could earn enough to buy half the amount of sausage, maybe more. But the truth is, I enjoy making sausages. I love to see the look on the faces of my family as they devour them, I love the idea that there is no better nourishment, that these sausages are wholesome and tasty and not unhealthy in any way. And I love being able to link them and to show off a little. Nothing beats that feeling when the freezer is full of the sausages I have made and we have breakfasts and other meals for a month.

Making sausages links me to the past. I cannot underestimate this, especially when it comes to making something like the Toulouse, or the Lucanian (I worry about Roman fish sauce, but you can get approximations for this in Lucanian sausage making). I don't go so far as to clean out my animal skins, just as in the same way I don't walk around in animal skins, but there is a link, an enjoyment to be had in the realisation that you are making something eaten thousands of years ago.

I remain fascinated with how people used to live, and for me this is a major motivation in sausage making. You will doubtless have your own motivations, but knowing I can make food, that if the whole world goes mad and there isn't a sausage to be had in the shops even for real money, I can make my own. As we say here in the North, 'There's nowt like knowing how!'

Getting started in sausage making

There is only one thing you need for making sausage – ingredients! Of course, like everything else in life, there is a multitude of equipment you can buy, some of it essential for certain tasks, some not so. But it is possible to make skinless sausages with nothing more than some meat, breadcrumbs and salt. For this you only need ordinary kitchen equipment. When you come to think of it, sausage making goes a long way into history, well before we had sausage stuffers, emulsifiers and collagen skins, so if they could do it 900 years ago with not much in the way of equipment, we can today!

Salt

Salt is a fundamental sausage making ingredient. The word 'sausage' actually means salted. Salt is the main preservative in sausages, but as we have already read there are lots of different kinds of salt.

Common table salt

It is possible to use table salt to make sausages but you do get an inferior product, both in terms of the preserving effect of the salt and the colour and flavour. Used at a rate of between 1.5 and 2.3

per cent of the meat content, salt prevents meat from being spoilt by microbes in a number of ways. Firstly, it is poisonous and interferes with the metabolism of the microbe. Secondly, it is osmotically powerful, drawing water from cells and often rupturing them in the process.

Ordinary kitchen salt contains substances to enable it to flow steadily, and other ingredients such as iodine. For this reason some sausage makers and home curers use kosher salt, which is additive-free.

Curing salt – a better salt than common table salt

The word botulism, originally Latin for sausage, is translated as 'sausage disease' and this problem is more or less alleviated by the use of saltpetre in your mix. What saltpetre actually is and how it is used varies according to where you are in history.

Once called Chinese Salt, it was used in the manufacture of gunpowder. It was usually collected from guano (bird or bat droppings), but in Europe it was collected from the soil beneath domestic toilets. Chemically, saltpetre is potassium nitrate, KNO^3 adding extra protection to common salt, NaCl (or sodium chloride). It also reacts with proteins, particularly what remains of the haemoglobin in meat, to give the product a pink hue.

How to use saltpetre in your sausage mix

First of all it is almost impossible to mix saltpetre crystals into salt in anything like the correct amount. Usually it is done at home, dissolved in water. The amount of saltpetre is tiny in comparison with the other ingredients and you will not get the mixing right, no matter how hard you try.

In America and most of Europe they talk about Prague Powder #1 and #2. The former has potassium nitrite added and the latter has both nitrite and nitrate. You have to add this in the right amount, depending on the recipe, and then also add an appropriate amount of salt. It is usually dyed pink, and so they call it 'pink salt'.

In the UK we are fortunate in having curing salt, with

everything mixed in as we need it. For those new to curing and sausage making, I suggest you stick to curing salt as you simply cannot go wrong. After 15 years of making sausage I still prefer to use ready-mixed curing salt because it is easy to use, foolproof and very safe.

Why is it better than ordinary salt?
The answer is simply because it kills more spoiling microbes, especially botulism bacteria. There is talk of it causing cancer in lab mice who have been fed inordinate amounts but in truth, botulism will kill you more quickly. But you don't need to take my word for it. If you wish, just use ordinary salt. There are plenty of sausage makers, some professional ones, who use only a little salt and treat the product as though it was fresh meat, cooking within a few days or alternatively, freezing, and advising their customers to do the same.

Getting the saltiness right
I make a batch of sausage meat and before stuffing into a skin I cook a small amount to see if the seasoning is acceptable. If it is too salty you can either add more ingredients or add a little sugar, which slightly disguises the salt but will not make up for really badly over-salted sausage.

I always start at 1 per cent, aiming for 1.25 per cent overall, and then test, adding a little more as I go.

Using the right percentage of salt
The amount of salt you add should be in proportion to the meat because that's what we are preserving, more or less. So a kilo of meat will start with 1 per cent, or 10g salt, which is 2 level teaspoons. After testing I might add more salt, making 1.25 per cent or sometimes even higher.

I add the salt to the liquid, usually water. That way it gets evenly distributed, and before stuffing I leave the well-mixed sausage meat to stand in the fridge for some hours so the flavours and salt can permeate the whole batch properly.

Using sausage skins

Making sausage in a skin is another skill to be learned in the kitchen. It is the unknown that puts people off making sausages – can they handle the skin, can they even buy skins? And not all skins are the same; they are categorised according to type, which animal they came from or if they were manmade, and their thickness and size. There is a difference between thickness and size. The size is how wide the tube is, the thickness is of the material used to make the tube.

It is more correct to refer to the skins of sausages as casings, since they are not always skin. You can buy manmade casings made from collagen, but even these are not vegetarian, being made from reconstituted animal protein. There has been talk of cellulose skins to make vegetarian sausages, mashed potato, cheese and onion, etc., but they are very difficult to use and all but impossible to get hold of.

The general animal casings we use in sausage making are beef, pig (mostly known as 'hog skins') and sheep skins. On top of this, skins have different sizes depending on which part of the alimentary canal they come from. Obviously the stomach is much bigger than the small intestine, and the 'skin' is thicker too. This affects what is known as the 'bite' of the sausage. Big fat sausages (yes, I know it's not a scientific term) have a greater resistance to the tooth when biting into the sausage than a thin collagen sausage.

Sausage casings are categorised as follows:
• Collagen – casings from 19 mm wide to 28 mm in diameter. These skins are not to be soaked in water before use (more on this later); they are straight in nature. Whenever you buy a straight sausage (without a natural bend in it), it is a manmade casing.

• The smaller skins are for cocktail sausages, the larger ones for German-type sausages that are often boiled. You can get coloured versions of the same skins, for making European sausages such as polony (Bologna) and kielbasa.

• Sheep – skins from 18–24 mm in diameter. Sheep skins are a more delicate bite than the other animal skins, but still very strong and used for sausage-like party bites and thin breakfast sausages. They need to be washed for some time so wash your sausage skins in about three or four changes of water over an hour period in a small bowl. At first they will have a strong aroma, which goes away in the washing process.

• Hog (pork) – skins come in a range of sizes, from 22–34 mm. Medium bite, the most common variety is about 24 mm in diameter. They are the fundamental skin for the typical 'banger', but the larger ones are used for sausages like boerewors and chorizo.

• Beef – skins come in sizes from 40 mm up to 80 mm and are heavy bite. They are used for all kind of sausage, from black pudding, using what are called 'runners' at 40 mm to haggis, using skins called 'bungs' or 'caps' at 80 mm.

New skin types
There are two forms of skin, tied or spooled. Until recently all skins were tied to a ring, packed in salt and sealed in a bag. Recently, spooled skins have become popular, that is a skin that is loaded onto a tube, having been salted. The tube allows you to more easily transfer your skin to the delivery tube of your sausage stuffer, but don't imagine the tube on which the skins are spooled makes a good loader. The majority of sausage making at home uses machines not powerful enough to force the meat through the tube.

How to handle sausage skins
All sausage skins are packed in salt, and need to be soaked in several changes of cool water to remove the salt and make the skin supple. The washing also removes any remaining smell. Having finished your batch of sausages, the remaining skins can be re-salted and stored in a plastic box in the fridge. Resalted

sausage skins that are completely encased in salt and will last indefinitely.

Though quite tough, make sure you handle sausage skins with care. Maybe the first time you get to use them they will feel somewhat strange, but try to overcome your squeamishness. If you have long fingernails you might tear the skin, but this is actually quite difficult to do.

In order to load onto the delivery tube you need to find the end of the tube. Spooled tubes are easy because you simply pull the skin from the tube. Tied skins are different: hold the ring and lift out of the water. The skins will fall over each other, a natural inbuilt consequence of their role in the gut. Finding the end of the tube is comparatively easy, opening it to load onto the stuffer is another thing altogether. I find it easier to place my finger at the final centimetre of the tube then pull the whole thing back over my finger, so the tube is now enveloping it. It can then be transferred to the delivery tube.

The majority of shop-bought sausages come from machine-loaded stock, often using collagen skins and generally the sausage is not linked in the traditional way. Indeed, many such sausages are simply compression cut, leaving the ends of the tube open. The contents of such sausages often include gelling agents to keep the cooking sausage from spilling out.

Cereal

Cereal is not a bulking agent. It is an important part of the sausage, which absorbs the cooking juices from the fat and meat, making the sausage succulent and flavoursome. Without cereal the juices in the sausage would pool when cooked, giving you a shrivelled piece of meat pate, usually quite hard, with liquid surrounding it, which escapes down your chin when you eat it.

What kind of cereal?

To be honest, I prefer breadcrumbs because they are always to hand, I don't need to buy them and they are not too strong a flavour (see page 29 for instructions on making fresh breadcrumbs). I don't know why but I dislike the flavour of rusk, which is the cereal of choice for most butchers and sausage makers.

There are good reasons for using rusk, though: it is yeast free. Breadcrumbs can reduce the keeping properties of sausages because the yeast ferments the sugars. This isn't a problem where the sausages are to be cooked and eaten soon afterwards, or frozen but sausages destined to spend a week on a shelf at 5°C (41°F) can deteriorate more quickly if made with breadcrumbs.

Rusk can also be gluten-free, and you can get other cereals that will do the same job, too. Combinations of ground rice and oatmeal work well, but you have to experiment to ascertain their water absorption properties.

A novel method of introducing cereal into sausages is to use Weetabix. This is brilliant for adding to sausages because it breaks down very easily to a mush, yet retains its absorption properties when it comes to flavour in the cooking sausage. Simply weigh out the appropriate amount and crumble into the mixture.

Water

Possibly one of the most important parts of the sausage, water is fundamentally there to distribute the salts and flavours around the sausage evenly by osmosis but more importantly, it has two other functions. The first is quite obvious: without being wet and pasty, the sausage meat will not easily stuff into the skin.

Secondly, and perhaps most importantly, the liquid in a sausage cooks it. If you think about it, a sausage is made of ground meat and breadcrumbs, and this combination makes a wonderful insulator. The water in the sausage cooks it by steaming from the inside.

Now you don't have to use just water. When making pork and apple sausages, I add apple juice and a venison sausage recipe I adore has red wine in it. I make a note of the ingredients of the liquids I am using since I don't want additives in my sausage beyond the ones I am using myself. Sometimes the liquid might come from a tin of tomatoes or passata, depending on the recipe.

Knowing how much liquid to use

As a general rule, sausages should have about 15 per cent liquid added. The actual amount is not completely critical, and this is down to the 'squidge' test. When you make your sausage meat, if you can't squidge it through your fingers, it is too dry so add a little extra liquid to make it flow.

Adding flavours

You can add all kinds of flavours to your sausage, from herbs to spices. Thyme, sage, onion, chives and garlic are the main flavours added to sausages, mostly adding to their keeping properties as well as flavour.

Paprika is a widely used flavour, but as you read through this book you will find there are umpteen flavours to be added to the sausage, remembering that the main flavour is meat. You cannot compare a 70 per cent pork sausage to a 40 per cent one, you will be so very impressed with a homemade sausage.

Fresh versus dried herbs and spices

Often dried herbs and spices are more concentrated than fresh ones, which seems a little counterintuitive. If a recipe calls for fresh herbs, and all you have is the dried version, use about half as much. Some herbs change in flavour or are changed in processing. For example, onion salt is clearly salty, but the oniony nature is somewhat different, too. A lot of sausage recipes call for onion and substituting onion salt will not only change the saltiness of the sausage, but it might not have the same flavour. It is much the same with garlic. Using garlic purée rather than fresh garlic will increase the salt content of the sausage and the garlic flavour will be somewhat different.

The answer is to experiment and get to know your ingredients. What works for you might not work for someone else, and that's one of the fun things about making your own sausages – getting it just right.

Funnel stuffer

Eventually you are going to want to make skin-stuffed sausages, and yet you can still do the job with very little equipment. For small batches of sausage you can buy a funnel stuffer. These come in various sizes and materials from plastic to porcelain, and cost very little. The sausage skin is loaded onto the delivery tube of the stuffer and the sausage meat loaded into the hopper. You use your thumbs to push the meat through the hopper (I say hopper, it really is the business end of a funnel) and into the skin. With this method you can easily make a metre of sausage and should you need more, simply reload more skins and carry on. They are ideal for using collagen skins, which require no soaking and just sit on the tube.

Blender/Food processor

When we talk about grinders we will discuss passing meat through different cutting plates to achieve certain textures in the sausage. When you simply want a smooth paste you can use a food processor. Indeed, you can also achieve a certain level of texture by pulsing your food processor. The action of the machine mixes too, but to rely on this you need a large machine with the capacity to make several kilos of mix, which is perhaps not available to the home sausage maker.

The food processor has one drawback in as much as it can get warm, and heat up the mixture. Even a degree or so can be unwanted. When I make sausages in this way I always try to use iced water, or crushed ice to keep the mixture as cool as possible.

Grinder (mincer)

Of course some food processors come with stuffing attachments but I prefer to use an old-fashioned meat grinder with a sausage stuffing attachment. You can buy a plastic meat grinder for very little money or spend quite a lot for a motorised version. All of them have basically the same layout and are almost interchangeable in design.

They come in sizes from a No. 4, which is very small to a No. 32, which is industrial in nature. The majority of home sausage makers use a No. 8, which is about the size of a bag of sugar.

One thing you need to consider when purchasing a hand grinder is the way it fastens to the work surface. Usually they are secured in place with a screw G clamp (sometimes known as a C clamp in the States) that is part of the moulding of the machine. This design has not changed since the time when everyone did their cooking preparation on a kitchen table. These days, of course, people use all kinds of surfaces to prep their food, and a G clamp doesn't always fit the modern work surface.

At home we have both work surfaces and a table. The G clamp on all of our grinders does not fit the table, so a notch had to be cut out of the table to make it fit! Obviously this would not do for the kitchen with only modern work surfaces, but there is another option. There are on the market some grinders that have suckers to attach them to a work surface. They are usually good enough to grind lean meat, but often fall down when it comes to fat and skin. You need a more robust machine for something like belly pork but, in conjunction with a blender, they make excellent sausage stuffers.

The grinder comes in seven parts. The outer casing is usually made of metal and has a delivery hopper at the top. I always put this in the freezer before use to cool it so the meat when it passes through does not warm up. It doesn't have to be completely freezing, but cooler than 5°C (41°F).

Inside fits the auger, which is a screw that pushes the meat forward and at the same time turns the cutting blade that fits at the end. The opposite end fits the handle, which is usually quite long to give you as much mechanical advantage as possible.

At the opposite end to the handle fits the cutting blade, usually onto a spigot on the auger, which abuts to a cutting plate. This in turn fits into a notch on the casing to prevent it from turning. The action of the blade against the plate cuts the meat while it is being forced through the holes on the cutting plate.

You usually get more than one, often three, cutting plates with increasingly small holes in them. This is to vary the fineness of the minced meat that comes out – the larger the holes, the rougher the cut. The whole thing is then held in place with a large locking nut.

When mincing meat with the grinder, the plate and cutting blade is in place. When using the machine to stuff sausage skins, the largest cutting plate (the one with the biggest holes) is used but no cutting blade. Between the casing and the outer fastening nut the sausage delivery tube is attached. Your sausage meat is fed into the hopper and forced out into the skins with a regular turning of the driving handle.

Electrically powered grinders

The only difference between a hand-powered grinder and an electrically powered one is that the power is supplied by an electric motor. Since the motor is usually quite large it is a much bigger machine that is stand-alone, with no G clamp to fix it anywhere.

The hopper is usually a large affair, which sits on the top of the machine. It has a large capacity and will allow you to simply drop the material at a much faster rate than a hand-cranked machine. It is not unusual to find powered machines dealing with 5 kilos of meat in a couple of minutes.

Sausage delivery tubes

I have bought some machines that come with a single delivery tube, and others that come with three, of various sizes from about 6 mm to about 2 cm. Obviously you choose the appropriate tube for the sausage skin you are stuffing. Metal tubes are much easier to use than plastic ones, and easier to clean too. However, most machines come with plastic tubes, which have a tendency to become furry after a while and therefore increasingly harder to stuff with. That nitpick over, there is not much else to say about them.

Gravity stuffer

If you are making a sausage that is rather fluid in texture, such as black pudding, you can use a gravity stuffer, which is more or less a funnel attached to a frame. The large skins are attached to the delivery tube and the material, which usually resembles a bowl of rough porridge, is fed through the hopper. It is a good idea to use these stuffers for making black pudding rather than using a cup over a bowl because it is much less messy.

Obviously, when making black pudding the skin, mostly beef runner skins, is knotted at the end first. I tend to avoid knotting ordinary sausages at the beginning of stuffing, allowing the air to escape through the open skin.

Push-fed stuffers

There are a lot of these in use, particularly in butchers and delis. You can buy domestic versions, especially if you make large batches of sausage. The domestic ones are fixed with a G clamp and consist of a piston that sits inside a cylinder. The piston is pushed forward by a screw turned by a handle and out into the sausage delivery tube.

Using these machines it is possible to get a very evenly filled sausage in comparatively little time. Usually they hold about 5 kg sausage meat (I use one for for chorizo making); the stuffing is stopped by releasing the pressure on the piston.

Of course there are a number of powered versions for professional use which churn out miles of sausage, using specially spooled skins.

Choosing the right machine

This isn't always an easy thing to do because there are so many factors involved, not the least one being your budget.

Buying a second-hand stuffer

You will find many second-hand grinders/stuffers on the internet. Personally I would avoid the older versions. They might well have a lot of life left in them, but you cannot guarantee the cutters are still sharp, the plates are not rusty and the auger and casings are not rusted either. If you have to buy an older second-hand machine then be sure to ask the seller questions about these parts.

You also need to be aware that the cutter and plate might be of a size no longer available, and this will render the machine useless for grinding. Ask if the sausage delivery tubes are still with the machine, as these are usually the first things to be mislaid.

Then there are new machines that sell for comparatively little money. Try to find out about the G clamp, if there are sausage delivery tubes and if they are standard-sized cutters. Many of these products come from China, and my experience of them is that the workmanship can be somewhat shoddy.

When it comes to buying electric machines, a whole new set of problems is introduced. I would avoid buying any machine substantially cheaper than those sold by mainstream butchers' suppliers.

I once had a pupil on one of our sausage making courses who had bought a machine over the internet for little money. It refused to stuff, though it did come with sausage stuffers. The problem was the machine needed a ring between the sausage stuffer and the flange of the delivery tube. This vital piece of equipment was not mentioned in the instructions, and only became apparent by careful study of the photograph on the box. Obviously there was no sign of the article in the box, and we had to fashion one from some plastic to make it work at all. But then the motor made a strange noise and after a few goes it decided not to continue in its task, and the machine was never used again.

If you want to buy a powered grinder/sausage stuffer then the best advice is to save up and buy one worth its salt from a reputable dealer you can return it to, should anything go wrong. Virtually the same goes for a mechanical grinder, which at current 2014 prices should cost around £30 and will last a lifetime as you will be able to buy spares as you go along. How many sausages do you need to make this money back? Well, if you made sausages once a month it would take about six months, so it's money well spent.

Other equipment

Knives

A selection of sharp knives is a must for any good kitchen application. In former years sausages were made from stuffing material that was literally bashed by two sets of knives on a block, as though the maker was playing the drums.

Chopping mats

A good mat for meat preparation, being red in colour, is a must for an easy-clean surface that protects the table. The largest one you can accommodate is best. Of course best practice is to have a number of boards coloured accordingly:

Red = raw meat
Blue = raw fish
Yellow = cooked meat
Green = salad and fresh fruit
Brown = vegetables
White = bread and bakery products

Scales, measuring jug/food thermometer

It is really important to have a way of weighing small amounts of dry powders like salt. It is possible to use a teaspoon for salt itself, since a level teaspoon holds 5 g salt but you can't easily do this for pepper or any number of dried herbs. A scale that will give the ability to measure a gram is really useful. Similarly, an accurate measuring jug is equally important. While we are on the subject of measuring, a good food thermometer is a must, too. If your kitchen scales do not weigh in increments of 1 g, then I would urge you to invest in some new digital scales. Alternatively, follow these suggested equivalents:

	Salt	Other spices
1 g	⅕ level tsp	⅓ level tsp
1.58 g	¼ level tsp	½ level tsp
2 g	⅓ level tsp	⅔ level tsp
3 g	⅔ level tsp	1 level tsp

A word about safety and cleanliness
Over the years I must have made thousands of sausages, and hopefully I will make many thousands more. This book is a guide to how I make sausages for my own family and how to make some really excellent food for very little money; also how it feels to go through the various processes of making sausages.

Writing a book that people will use to make food for their families is quite a responsibility. It is my hope that you will enjoy the recipes in this book, and that you will be encouraged to make sausages and concoct recipes of your own. Also, that you will look up recipes on the internet and have the confidence to follow them, and more to the point, have the ability to spot when they are likely to be very good, or alternatively, not so good. Of course part of the responsibility in writing this book is to ensure you stay safe when eating sausages that you have made. With this in mind, make sure you follow these basic rules:

Cleanliness
Be scrupulously clean, disinfecting everything that comes into contact with your meat, ingredients and products. Wear appropriate clothing too. In the home environment this means an apron and if you have long hair, at least tie it back, remove any rings and make sure your hands are thoroughly washed. It is important that you take every precaution to make sure your food is completely safe by having a cleanliness regime that works.

Coolness
Always chill your meat, and keep it chilled the whole time, from the point of purchase to the point of cooking. Use chilled water in the sausage recipes to keep the meat cool as you work. This reduces the ability of spoiling organisms to reproduce in the product and therefore lessens the chances of dangerous spoilage. Whenever you are not actually working on your product, keep it in a cold fridge.

Do not allow meat to warm to a temperature greater than 5°C (41°F) unless you are fermenting a sausage.

Storage

Unless hanging to ferment your sausages, treat them just like fresh meat and store them in the fridge for up to five days, or freeze them. Store sausages for cooking in the fridge in a covered container (either a bowl with a plate or a plastic-lidded box). Do not store for longer than five days before cooking unless otherwise indicated by the recipe. If you are going to freeze them, make sure you do so at the earliest possible moment and no longer than 24 hours after production. To freeze sausages, pack in freezer bags and label them with the recipe title and date. If you can vacuum pack your sausages they will keep even better.

Cooked sausage may be covered and stored in the fridge for a few days only.

Salt

In the recipes that follow, always use curing salt unless otherwise indicated. This is not generally available from supermarkets but it can easily be purchased on the internet and is comparable in price to ordinary salt. Do not skimp on the salt quantities stated. The sausages in this book are all low in salt because I follow a low-salt diet. Commercially-produced sausages do have a lot of salt in them, often far too much, and require sugar to disguise their flavour. These recipes are much less salty, but nonetheless, with every sausage you make, test a sample first before stuffing into skins and adjust the salt accordingly.

Chapter 2

Making sausages for the first time

Anyone can make sausages

This section is divided into two parts, the theory and the recipes. I have separated the theory from the recipes so that you can get an idea of the thought processes behind these sausages and understand the basic point that sausages do not need to be in a skin and sausage making does not require lots of equipment. Sausages are simple rustic foods that take on the form of delicacies in the right hands.

There are a number of ways you can make sausages without having to buy or learn how to use the numerous tools of the sausage making fraternity. Among the many questions we are constantly asked, one that pops up with a degree of regularity is how to make vegetarian sausages. Until recently this has been an almost impossible task because sausage skins are animal products, and even manmade sausage skins are formed from reconstituted animal protein, making them unsuitable for vegetarians. However, after much experimentation, we have developed a number of ways of making both vegetarian and non-vegetarian sausages in the kitchen without the need for skins.

Making simple skinless sausages

It is possible to create sausages that you just roll out as a sausage shape. In order to make sure these sausages do not fall to pieces there are a number of things you can do. Firstly, adding rather more liquid than you would normally use allows the sausage to be bound more completely but then the addition of some dry ingredients, such as fennel seeds or finely chopped cucumber strips or shredded chives, serves to hold the meat together rather like straw in mud when making houses from wattle and daub.

There are lots of recipes for such sausages, including beef and onion, or pork and apple. Cutting your apple into small 2.5 cm strips as thinly as possible, mixed with the meat still gives the exact amount of flavour, and you simply will not notice any alteration of texture either.

The same goes for more traditional pork sausages. For example, making a skinless pork sausage with breadcrumbs, salt and pepper and water stuffed in a skin is easy enough, but to recreate the skinless version is just as simple. I nearly always use some belly pork in my pork sausage because the fat portion is just perfect and the skin gives a brilliant flavour. Use a very sharp knife to cut some cabbage into very thin strands, let's call them shoelaces, about 5 cm long, and add this to the meat mixture to create a rolled sausage that is strong enough to hold its shape while cooking, either frying or baking, and so retain its sausage status.

The same goes for beef and tomato sausage. Pieces of finely sliced tomato will bind the sausage; the tendency is just to purée the tomato in the sausage but this is not quite good enough when creating a skinless sausage.

Using egg as a binding agent

There are some sausages that need a little help in staying together but you can create a sausage that sets with a reasonable stiffness by incorporating egg into the mix. You only need one egg per kilo, and this should be beaten first before adding to the mixture. The typical process would be to make your sausage meat first, and then fold in the egg to the mixture before cooking. Do not use the food processor, as this will introduce air into the sausage.

Using egg as a binding agent is useful for making sausages that will eventually find their way into a casserole since the binding keeps the integrity of the sausage and prevents it from falling apart during cooking.

Vegetarian skinless sausages

There are a number of possibilities here. Obviously you are not able to create sausages using animal skins at all, but you can make skinless ones. Actually, you can make skinned sausages, but more about that later in this chapter.

The kind of vegetarian you are will determine which possibilities you can have. For a start, meat substitutes do act somewhat like minced meat, and with the combination of this, breadcrumbs and some liquid you will have a very acceptable sausage. To make a vegetarian sausage takes a little more to help it along. If you can use them, an egg makes a good binding agent, but you can also use agar agar or carrageen.

Like gelatine, agar agar or carrageen are setting agents which add no flavour but do hold food together. They come from seaweed and you simply follow the instructions on the packet. Simply mix into the water portion of the recipe mix before rolling out, then let the material set.

Where vegetarian sausages really come into their own is the numerous skin alternatives you can use, from lettuce leaf to a single sheet of filo pastry. This material is vegan and if you imagine a sausage roll, with the pastry reduced so much that it contains only a single sheet, rather than cooking crisp, they cook soft, almost exactly like a sausage skin. The only difference is the overall shape of the sausage.

Conventional non-vegetarian sausages are cooked under pressure. The skins become taut as the 'meat' of the sausage inside – particularly the steam from the liquid portion – expands in the sausage. This is what gives it a smooth, plump skin. However, a wrapped sausage does not have this. Instead the covering, be it a leaf or a sheet of pastry, actually takes the form of the meat within it so whereas it is possible to make a sausage, it is usually a somewhat knobbly one.

Slicing sausage alternatives

It is possible to make some brilliant slicing sausages, such as liver sausage, chorizo, polony of various types, kielbasa ... the list is endless. All you need to do is create your meat and then wrap it in Clingfilm, lots of it, turned tightly at the ends and then boil it. Once cooled, these sausages are really acceptable and you would go a long way to find any difference between them and the shop-bought product.

Traditionally many of these sausages are air-dried, but by using this method you can make a version that approximates to the traditional sausage, but at the same time is not going to be too cumbersome or difficult a process.

Other skin alternatives

You can buy moulds made from silicone that allow you to make perfect sausage shapes using your own meat or a vegetarian alternative, or a concoction of your own making. These sausages do not have to be skinned at all, you simply load your meat into the silicone mould (often there are about a dozen sausages in each mould) and then you cook them straight away in the oven. Alternatively you can put the mould into the freezer straight away and when frozen, transfer them to a bag.

Moulded sausages need a little help to stay together once cooked, using gelatine, agar agar or carrageen. These setting agents are dissolved in the water portion of the recipe. Alternatively, any of the sausage recipes in this book will work well with the addition of a little egg.

Rossages

So what is the difference between a rissole and a sausage? Not a lot, really – you can make your sausage meat as you would normally, then dip in beaten egg and cover with breadcrumbs. That way you have a sausage with a difference. Rather than having to be baked in the oven, these sausages can also be fried in the traditional manner.

A similar sausage can be created by making your sausage meat and, in a separate bowl, rub in some fat and flour (see recipes below). Spread this mixture out on a baking tray and roll your sausages in it, so you have a sausage with a pastry coating that has not yet had any water added to bring it to a paste. This creates a sausage with a crumble-like outer surface that absorbs the cooking liquids from the meat.

Cooking sausages

Skinned sausages should never be pricked when cooking. Use a couple of tablespoons of light oil (I prefer rapeseed or sunflower) when frying and if you are able, use a probe thermometer to check the centre of the sausage is 75°C (167°F). Alternatively, cut into one sausage and inspect the contents, which should look cooked and not raw.

Baking should be done at 160–180°F (Gas 3–4) and should take around 30 minutes. Never cook a sausage under high heat; it simply browns the skin, leaving the insides dangerously uncooked.

Grill sausages on a low heat for around 20 minutes, turning often.

BBQ sausages should start on the coolest part of the BBQ for 15 minutes, turning often. Finish off in the hottest part for 5 minutes, again turning often.

Always check the cooking of your sausage, either by a thermometer – it should read 75°C (167°F) – or by inspection.

Recipes for simple, skinless sausages

The following three recipes are for simple, skinless vegetarian sausages. You can wrap them in filo of different thicknesses, or roll in breadcrumbs, having first dipped them in beaten egg.

I buy a packet of filo pastry and remove a single sheet, which is laid on a clean work surface and the stuffing piled in a ridge along the bottom. The pastry next to the stuffing is moistened with a brush of water, egg wash or milk and the whole sausage rolled over to form a seal. I then trim the pastry with a sharp knife and the next sausage can be made. When cooked in this way, the filo stays translucent and soft. If you add a number of sheets of filo the outer ones will crispen up in the cooking process, a bit like a sausage roll. It's up to you how many sheets to use.

When it comes to frying, a light oil is best. Generally I use a tablespoon of rapeseed or sunflower but hardly ever olive oil. My mother still uses lard to this day!

Mixed bean sausages
Makes 8 sausages

Mixed beans make great sausages. You can mash them, mix them with all kinds of flavours and they make a hearty meal. They are super with salads, roast meals, vegetarian or otherwise.

500 g cannellini and red kidney beans
300 g cooked white rice
1 small onion, finely chopped
1 garlic clove, crushed
1 level teaspoon chilli powder or chopped fresh red chilli
(add less if you prefer a milder flavour)
1 tablespoon sweet chilli sauce
1 level teaspoon salt
1 tablespoon potato flour
A little plain flour for dusting
A little oil for frying

1. First, cook the beans in boiling water for about 15 minutes until soft and cooked through.

2. Now place all the ingredients together in the bowl of a food processor and blend to a rough paste. It can be made as smooth as you prefer.

3. Roll into sausages. The rolling part is easy: lightly dust with plain flour and use your hands to shape the mixture into torpedos. You can vary this by rolling under a cutting board (a plastic lightweight one gives a more professional-looking finish). Roll long sausages and simply cut to the desired length.

4. Fry in a little oil to reheat or brush with oil and grill until golden. Serve immediately.

Cheese, courgette and red pepper sausages
Makes 5 sausages

You simply cannot beat the combination of flavours and textures in this sausage. It's super in a cold summer salad and magnificent served hot in a roll with mustard for a veggie hot dog.

A little oil for frying
1 medium onion, finely chopped
1 red pepper, deseeded and chopped
200 g grated courgettes
200 g grated Cheddar
1 medium egg, beaten
Salt and pepper to taste (remember, the cheese will be salty)
200 g freshly made breadcrumbs (see box below)

1. First, fry the onion in a little oil, adding the red pepper after just a few minutes. Add the grated courgettes and cook the mixture for 2–3 minutes more, stirring. Transfer to a bowl and leave to cool for 5 minutes.

2. Stir in the Cheddar with half the beaten egg and a little seasoning. Add 150 g of the breadcrumbs then mix well with your hands to combine.

3. Form the mixture into 5 sausage shapes. Dip in the remaining egg and then roll in the remaining breadcrumbs. Refrigerate covered until ready to eat (they will keep for five days).

4. Heat about a tablespoon of oil in a frying pan and fry gently for about 20 minutes until golden. Serve immediately.

How to make fresh breadcrumbs

There are lots of ways to do this. You can remove the crust from the appropriate amount of bread and dry in the oven on its lowest setting for a couple of hours. Afterwards blitz it in the food processor or grate it with a grater (if your bread goes red, you have cut your finger!). Alternatively, put it in a freezer bag, secure and bash with a rolling pin.

Leek and potato sausages
Makes 8 sausages

These sausages are wonderful with onion gravy and also make a fantastic addition to a Christmas or celebration dinner. However, the most tremendous meal can be made from some boiled fish served with these sausages, covered in caper sauce, or if you prefer serve with some corn on the cob smothered in butter.

Knob of butter
1 medium-sized leek, finely chopped
5 large baking potatoes, baked at 190°C (Gas 5) for 40 minutes until tender and cooled
100 g Gruyère or similar cheese, grated
1 garlic clove, chopped
1 tablespoon freshly chopped parsley
30 g breadcrumbs
Salt and pepper to taste
1 medium egg, beaten
2–3 tablespoons seasoned plain flour
A little oil for frying

1. First, fry the leek gently in the butter until soft but not brown. Leave to cool.

2. Scoop the potato flesh from the skins and place in a bowl. Add the cheese, garlic, parsley, breadcrumbs and leek. Season to taste and mix until well combined. If the mixture is too dry and crumbly, add a little beaten egg and mix again.

3. Form into sausage shapes and dip in beaten egg and then the flour. Place on a baking tray and chill for two hours before frying in a little oil until golden.

Meaty sausages

The variety of meat sausage we consume is huge. They have both historic and culinary significance. When you mention the word 'sausage', generally this is what comes to mind: a thick, juicy, succulent and meaty sausage!

Turkish-style sausages
Makes about 8 sausages

These sausages contain meat but they still do not need sausage skins. Similar to a kebab, they may be cooked on skewers if you wish.

400 g minced lamb
400 g minced beef
80 g bulgur wheat (add sufficient hot water to cover and leave for
10 minutes or according to the directions on the package)
1 small onion, sliced
1 red pepper, deseeded and sliced
3 garlic cloves
2 tablespoons pine nuts
2 teaspoons ground cumin
4 tablespoons fresh chopped parsley
10 g curing salt
1 teaspoon black pepper

1. Combine the meat in a bowl and mix in the bulgur wheat, (draining off the excess water) when cool. Place all the remaining ingredients in a food processor and blend until a paste is formed. Add a little water to loosen, if necessary.

2. Stir the paste into the meat, combining everything well. Massage the flavours into the meat to make a pliable mixture.

3. Form into sausage shapes about 10 cm long, moulding around skewers if you prefer. Leave covered on a baking tray for 1 hour (do not refrigerate) before grilling, frying or cooking on the barbecue.

Recipes for sausages with casings

When it comes to using animal casings, most people's first instinct is to recoil. After all, they are intestines. But with a little experience in handling skins, making sausages becomes not only simple but also packed with humour and fun. It is actually a very pleasant experience.

Making your first sausage in a skin

This is a sausage that we make for breakfast on a regular basis. It isn't difficult, and to be honest, it is made from whatever meat we can get. Sometimes it is pork shoulder, other times diced pork or minced pork, which makes the job even easier.

The following recipe is about as easy as it gets, and the things to remember are don't panic and always take your time. Also, remember the cardinal rules: cleanliness, keep the temperature cool and use the right amount of salt (see page 22).

Makes about 10 sausages

1 kg diced pork shoulder
150 ml water
12 g curing salt
150 g breadcrumbs
2 g ground black pepper
1 teaspoon mustard powder (as heaped as you dare but remember, it's hot and this is not a challenge!) or 1 teaspoon prepared mustard

Step 1
First of all, buy your meat. For this recipe you need 1 kg diced pork shoulder. Take a cool bag with you, or buy some ice cubes to pack the meat into so that you keep the meat as cold as possible.

Step 2
Back home, leave a jug of 150 ml water in the fridge to cool. Meanwhile, sterilise all your equipment. Boiling water works best for me but then I have to cool everything down. Milton

Sterilising Fluid also works well, especially for work surfaces, cutting boards, etc. All the bowls and trays you will be using need to be sterilised.

Step 3
Put your sausage skins in a bowl of cool water to soak for an hour, changing the water twice in that period. Simply leave them to soak and forget about them. Spooled skins are on a plastic tube to allow the skin to be easily transferred to the delivery tube on your stuffer. Loose sausage skins are simply tied to a ring so you can pick up the whole tangled mass of skins more easily.

If using spooled skins, you only need one spool for this quantity. However, if you are using salted skins that are not spooled, you will need to soak the lot unless you are prepared to unravel a dried and hard skin from the mass, cut it off and soak it. Don't worry about soaking all the skins, you can re-salt them.

If using dry, collagen skins, these don't need soaking at all and are perhaps easiest of all to load onto the stuffer.

Step 4
Assemble your grinder for mincing the meat. Put the metallic parts of the grinder (all of it really, unless it's made of plastic) in the freezer to cool down. If you can't do this, put them in the fridge, or soak in cold water.

Grind the sausage meat using the coarse plate according to the manufacturer's directions and collect the minced meat on a tray or in a bowl. Return the meat to the fridge.

Step 5
Prepare your breadcrumbs, salt, water and pepper. Add the salt to the water from the jug in the fridge, and add the pepper to the breadcrumbs and mix really well. Then add the mustard powder to the breadcrumbs. If using prepared mustard (English works best), add this to the meat and mix well.

Step 6
Wash your hands and use them to combine all the ingredients in the bowl, mixing until everything is uniform in colour and consistency.

Step 7
Now for the taste test … Check for seasoning by cooking a small amount of sausage mixture in a little oil. If it is not salty enough, add a little more in ¼ teaspoon amounts. If the mixture is too salty for you, add more breadcrumbs and a teaspoon of sugar.

Repeat cooking and tasting, as necessary, until you are happy.

Step 8
The squidge test … Will the mixture easily stuff into a skin? You can decide for yourself.

Step 9
Now load your sausage delivery tube onto your stuffer/grinder according to the manufacturer's directions.

Step 10
Load the delivery tube with your skins. Pull a little of the skin over the end of the tube so that when the meat comes through it will fill the skin and drag the length of skin off the tube as it fills. Do not knot the skin or you'll just get a bubble – you can knot it at the end of the process.

Step 11
As the sausage skin fills, keep reloading the hopper. Eventually you will run out of meat but there will be some remaining in the sausage machine and delivery tube. To remove this, force a piece of bread through the machine and this will push out the very last bit of sausage.

As the sausage is being delivered the skins might start to dry out, so make sure you keep them moist with a little water applied with your fingertips.

Avoid overstuffing the sausage by maintaining an even pressure with the crank (if using a hand grinder) and if necessary, have someone else there to keep up a bit of negative pressure on the sausage skin too by pulling it.

Step 12
Pull or slice off any remaining skin to leave yourself with about 7 cm to tie a knot. Knot both ends of the sausage and trim away any excess.

Step 13
To make the links, take the stuffed skin in both hands. With each hand hold the sausage between the thumb, first and second fingers. You are now holding the sausage with just three fingers of each hand. Move your fingers so the left and right hand fingers are almost touching. Squeeze the sausage with the fingers of each hand to make a little indentation, then twist the sausage to form the link, twisting about three times.

Step 14
If you wish to keep the sausages for more than a few days, freeze them (page 21). Otherwise, cover with foil, Clingfilm or place in a liddled plastic box then leave them in the fridge overnight for the flavours to develop. Cook slowly and enjoy!

Alternative methods
Some people make sausages in different ways and perhaps there are as many ways of making sausage as there are sausage makers! Some grind their meat coarsely, mix this with the other ingredients and then regrind using a finer grinding plate. Still others don't bother with a second grinding. Actually, some don't bother to grind at all, buying minced meat from the butcher or supermarket and just making do with that. I must confess that this is a popular method, but you don't get really smooth sausages, which doesn't matter if you are not looking for a smooth product but most people would recognise this as a quality sausage.

The three-fold link

To start, you need a skin of sausage meat with about 5–8 cm unfilled skin. Now make an indentation by using the thumb, forefinger and second finger of each hand, one sausage length from the end of your first sausage filling (i.e. from the start of the wobbly bit of unfilled skin). Make a twist link there.

Take hold of the unfilled skin and bring it round the link. Tie it off at the link so you now have a pair of sausages and a long tube of sausage. Make another indentation in the long tube of sausage the same length as the other two, and pull it round the link, having made an indentation, so you now have a trio of sausages. Attach to this a pair of sausages and then a long tube of sausage.

Repeat this last step to add the third sausage to the pair, and continue until the whole skin is used up.

Troubleshooting guide

Sometimes the whole sausage making process goes awry and you can end up in a bit of a mess. It must be said that most messes are caused by panic, so the first rule is to stay calm!

My early mistakes include soaking collagen skins, which become like tissue paper and simply fall apart when you try to stuff them; not being able to find the end of a hog skin while making a TV appearance and getting all hot under the collar; finding the skin was damaged by some form of impact that caused holes to appear every few centimetres along the sausage; and adding too much salt or too much liquid, paprika, water or pepper. Also, using 'off' meat, meat that had already been frozen and dropping all the sausages on the floor to be snatched up by a dog, who then needed veterinary care because he couldn't cope with all that raw pork!

What to do when ...

There are holes in your sausage skin

In this case you really can't do anything so store the meat in the fridge while you re-soak a different batch of skins. Only once have I had this problem: the skins were damaged by some impact and consequently they were all in the same condition. From then on I have always kept a supply of collagen skins to hand (no soaking required) just in case.

You add too much salt

So you've made a batch of sausage meat and are testing the stuff in a pan only to find that it's too salty. Clearly you need more ingredients. I tend to save a little meat for such a test, and of course extra breadcrumbs can be added. Failing this, you can add a cup of water and let it drain over a sterile colander. Adding a teaspoon of sugar often helps too.

The same goes for the addition of other flavours. If you have added too much, you need to cool the mixture down. Frequently, a little milk will do the trick. Add the milk in 50 ml quantities, checking to see if this has adequately cooled the sausage.

You can't get the skins on the delivery tube

Find the end by forcing your little finger through the side of the skin, to fold it in as it were, and you'll soon find the open end. Now dip the end in a little olive oil and add a few drops to the soaking water a few minutes before you need to load your skins.

It's hard to force the meat through the delivery tube

Simply add a little oil to the meat and if you have some low-calorie oil spray, squirt some up the tube to lubricate it a little.

Meaty recipes

Easy liverwurst
Makes 4 large sausages

A tasty sausage that is quite similar in flavour to a good pork pâté. You need about 2 m hog casings, soaked in water. Hog casings come in various sizes and for this recipe use 28 mm ones that give you a sausage that can be sliced and eaten with the skin, or squeezed and the contents consumed like a pâté.

1 kg pork liver, sliced
1.5 kg pork shoulder, chopped
1 medium onion, finely chopped
2 tablespoons salt
½–1 level teaspoon dried sage
1 level teaspoon marjoram
230 ml cold water

1. First, cook the pork liver gently in sufficient water to just cover. Cook for a few minutes until it changes colour but is still very tender. Mince the pork shoulder and liver together until very smooth and place in a bowl.

2. Add the onion, salt, sage, marjoram and water. Mix well, massaging the flavours into the meat.

3. Prepare the casings and your method of stuffing (page 32). Stuff the casings well with the meat mixture, making sure there are no air pockets. Note: the air pockets are just a nuisance but they won't burst. If you want to present a lovely sausage it shouldn't have air in it but it doesn't really matter if there are some present.

4. Link the sausages as required (page 35) and cook in simmering water for about 15 minutes. When cooked, leave to cool and eat sliced cold. You can freeze them as soon as they are cool enough to go in the freezer or vacuum pack and store in the fridge.

French-style garlic slicing sausage
Makes 18–20 sausages

One for garlic lovers, this is good on pizzas and with cheeses and salad. You will need about 2 m of large hog casings.

2 kg pork shoulder, minced
1 tablespoon salt
5 garlic cloves, finely chopped
½ tablespoon caster sugar
½ teaspoon white pepper
¼ teaspoon grated nutmeg
2 egg whites

1. Combine all the ingredients in a mixing bowl and massage into the meat with your hands. Do this for a few minutes so the meat is evenly flavoured with the garlic.

2. Prepare the casings and your chosen method of stuffing (page 32). Stuff the casings with the meat mixture, making sure as little air as possible is going through.

3. Link the sausages into 15–18cm lengths (page 35) and then simmer for 15 minutes in hot water.

4. Oven bake at 160°C/Gas 3 for about 25 minutes.

Lithuanian potato sausage
Makes about 15 sausages

This unusual potato-based sausage can be oven baked or simmered in a pan of salted water. The Lithuanian potato sausage is simply served in a stew like a Toulouse sausage cassoulet, or with heaps of boiled cabbage covered in pepper and melted butter. You will need 2 m of hog casings.

A little light oil
1 large onion, finely chopped
6 rashers streaky bacon, chopped
12 medium-sized potatoes
½ teaspoon dried marjoram
2 large eggs, beaten
2 teaspoons salt
Ground black pepper to taste
A little flour in a flour shaker (add to the mixture if it is too wet)
A little butter to grease

1. In a large frying pan fry the onion and bacon together in a little light oil until the onion has softened. Allow to completely cool. Meanwhile, peel and grate the potatoes, squeezing out most of the moisture before you transfer them to a mixing bowl. Add the onion and bacon mixture and combine.

2. Mix the marjoram into the beaten egg, stir well into the potato mixture and season with salt and pepper. Bring the mixture together with your hands and squeeze it out of your hands between your thumbs and forefingers. If it is too wet and squidgy, dust over a little flour from the shaker and mix well again.

3. Prepare the hog casings and method of stuffing (page 32) and push the potato mixture into the casings.

4. Bake in a buttered roasting tin for about 40–45 minutes in a preheated oven at 160°C/Gas 3 or place in a pan of simmering water for about 50–55 minutes.

Polony-style sausage
Makes about 15 large sausages

This style of sausage was once very popular in eighteenth and nineteenth-century Britain. The name is thought to originate from one of two sources: Polonia, the old name for Poland, or Bologna in Italy – both being famous for their sausages.

The Polony is the great peasant sausage of Eastern Europe, with enormous variety in content and texture. Sometimes very fatty, sometimes rough textured, it is mostly very smooth. It can contain offal and meat mixtures and is frequently highly spiced. Often it is served with rustic bread. You will need 2 m hog casings.

2.5 kg pork shoulder
500 g belly pork
1 tablespoon salt
1 level tablespoon curing salt
250 g rusk or breadcrumbs
1 teaspoon white pepper
¼ teaspoon each of grated mace, nutmeg, coriander and cinnamon

1. First, mince the two meats together until very finely ground and transfer to a bowl. Sprinkle over the salt and curing salt; mix well. Cover and leave in the fridge for 2 hours.

2. Add the rusk or breadcrumbs to the meat and mix well. In a separate dish, add the pepper and spices; mix well. Sprinkle over the meat and mix together well with your hands. The mixture needs to be very smooth so use a food processor to blend to a smooth paste (do this in small batches).

3. Prepare the casings and method of stuffing (page 32). Fill the casings with the meat mixture. Simmer in a pan of boiling water for about 30–35 minutes.

4. Cover and leave to dry in a cool place for about 12 hours.

Chapter 3

British sausages and how to make them

This chapter looks at the various sausages produced in the UK, how they differ, one from the other, and how to make them. There is much confusion about many sausages and I suppose it is possible you will never actually get to the bottom of some origins. Suffice to say that most sausages we have in the UK have an origin somewhere, but perhaps their destination is more important!

As previously stressed, it is important to work in a spotlessly clean environment, with all utensils sterilised and all ingredients as fresh and cool as possible. Store your meat in the fridge and pop the grinder in the freezer before use (see also page 33). Note: some recipes add around 100 g breadcrumbs and a little water to bind the ingredients. Using this method, don't pound the ground sausage with the pestle and mortar, just finely grind all the ingredients and add a little water to make the mixture more pliable.

Chipolatas
These are often mistaken for what might be called cocktail sausages, which are only half the length. Indeed the chipolata was a British sausage long before they were known as such. They are typical of sausages made in a country where sheep are common, since they are stuffed into sheep casings, and Britain was always the world's capital for sheep.

The actual word is French or Italian in origin, and possibly came to the UK when the Huguenots arrived there in the sixteenth century. It means 'made or cooked with onion'. Chipolatas are sausages stuffed into sheep skins about 18 mm in diameter. They are usually about 12–18 cm long, so reasonably long and thin. You cannot get hog skins of this diameter and so you have to use sheep.

Essentially a London sausage, chipolatas are sometimes smoked and contain no breadcrumbs. The meat is very finely pounded with all the other ingredients, and the various recipes for chipolata sausages use different a combinations of meats and spices.

The Christmas dish 'pigs in blankets', which is a sausage wrapped in bacon, is said to be made with chipolatas, but these days one usually finds them with much larger sausages.

Basic chipolatas
Makes 12 sausages

These flavours can be augmented – try a teaspoon of mustard powder, or sage or thyme. For this recipe you will need a pestle and mortar. Sterilise equipment prior to use and cool as much in the freezer as possible (see also page 33).

900 g belly pork
700 g pork shoulder
1 heaped tablespoon fresh rosemary
1 level tablespoon salt
15 g white pepper
15 g onion powder (or replace with a medium onion chopped finely and gently sweated in a little oil)
sausage skins

1. Put your sausage skins in some cold water to soak. Every 15 minutes change the water and after an hour they should be ready. Meanwhile, put the pestle and mortar in the fridge to cool.

2. Roughly chop the meat and grind with the large plate according to the manufacturer's dirctions. In a bowl mix all the ingredients together well and regrind the meat and flavourings with a fine plate. Place the sausage meat in a bowl covered in Clingfilm and refrigerate just to get the temperature down.

3. Take the meat in spoonfuls and pound to a paste with the mortar and pestle, making it as fine as possible. Stuff into the skins and tie off at around 15 cm (see also page 34). Note: sheep skins are quite tough and difficult to overfill. Leave overnight, in a bowl covered in Clingfilm or a lidded box for the flavours to develop, then fry slowly.

The breakfast sausage

The history of the full English breakfast is a little complex. Some authorities, including the TV presenter and countryside expert Jack Hargreaves, have argued that the British national dish is bacon and eggs because most people with a little room to spare kept both a pig and chickens. However, the full English includes sausage, tomato and fried bread. Purists would not include baked beans or hash browns, an American addition. In the north of the country the predominant sausage poor people ate on a regular basis was the black pudding. The addition of black pudding to the English breakfast is considered a step too far for some, particularly those in the south. But it is clear that northerners insist black pudding should be on the plate along with a breakfast sausage and the eggs and bacon.

Breakfast sausages have become a little bland these days but at one time they were far from tasteless, containing Tabasco, Worcestershire sauce or anchovy sauce. Victorian recipes abound for highly flavoured breakfast sausages. It is said they were particularly enjoyed by Queen Victoria, who would not eat sausages made in a grinder but insisted the meat be finely chopped with a knife.

Irish breakfast sausage
Makes about 12 sausages

Broadly speaking, the Irish sausage is similar to the Lincolnshire in as much as it has a lot of sage in it. You can reduce the amount of sage if you like, particularly if you only have dried sage, which is much more strongly flavoured.

These sausages contain precious little salt and I suggest you make the meat up first, then test a little to see if it is right for you (see also page 34). Either freeze or eat these sausages soon after making them. In other words, treat them like fresh meat. You will need 2 m of 22 mm hog skins for the casings.

1 kg pork shoulder
250 g pork fat (back fat, cut into small pieces of about 5 mm each)
150 g breadcrumbs
150 ml water
2 level teaspoons salt
25 g chopped fresh sage
1 level teaspoon pepper
½ teaspoon allspice

1. As before, sterilise everything prior to use and cool as much as possible in the freezer or fridge. (see also page 33).

2. Grind the pork shoulder with the large grinder plate according to the manufacturer's directions before combining all the ingredients and grinding on a fine plate. Transfer to a bowl and cover with Clingfilm.

3. Meanwhile, soak your skins for at least an hour in cool water, with several changes (see also page 33).

4. Load your skins onto the delivery tube of your grinder/stuffer and stuff as loosely as possibly with the sausage meat. Link (see page 35) and then leave in a bowl covered with Clingfilm in the fridge overnight to allow the flavours to develop before cooking or freezing.

Dinner sausages

The appellation 'dinner sausage' is a little vague because almost all sausages are suitable for consumption as a main or evening meal. They are characterised as having either strong flavours or being large in size (usually in diameter) and they have strong skins (usually 28 mm).

Dinner sausages are somewhat dual purpose in as much as the recipes for making meals with them are varied. You can eat them stand alone with vegetables, or frequently as part of a casserole. The archetypal sausage that fills both camps is the Toulouse.

Dinner sausages
Makes about 12 sausages

This is a basic French recipe, reasonably low in salt and fat. It is mildly spiced with pepper and garlic and usually cooked in a cassoulet but can be eaten in its own right. You will need 2 m of hog casings (22–28 mm in diameter), soaked in water for a good hour before use.

1 kg pork shoulder
500 g belly pork
200 g back fat
150 ml dry white wine

Seasonings
20 g curing salt
1 teaspoon white pepper
5 garlic cloves, crushed

1. First, sterilise all your equipment (see also page 32). Chill the meat and the grinder to as near to freezing point as you can without making the meat solid. This will take a couple of hours.

2. Meanwhile, cut the back fat into 5 mm cubes. Roughly grind the meat and incorporate with all the other ingredients in a bowl. For a more even mix, dissolve the salt in the wine first.

3. Stuff the sausage meat loosely into hog casings and then refrigerate overnight in a bowl covered with Clingfilm or a lidded plastic box before cooking.

Venison and pigeon

Venison is one of the least fatty meats you can buy, and these sausages have quite a lot of added fat. Pigeon is the perfect accompaniment to this meat, being highly blooded, which makes it dark and savoury. It makes for a sausage that is rich and flavoursome and the *al dente* nature of hog casings makes for a sausage that explodes in the mouth. However, the sausage meat could easily be stuffed into hog casings (or collagen for that matter) and sliced on the plate, perhaps with a portion of venison, pigeon and duck with a rich sauce.

Venison and pigeon sausages
Makes about 10 sausages

Use 4 m of sheep casings, soaked in water for a good two hours before use, or 2 m of hog casings (22–28 mm in diameter), soaked in water for a good hour before use.

Try serving with potato and swede mash and steamed celeriac. I have lightly fried the sausages in a little oil, then transferred them to the oven to finish off. Add a couple of finely chopped shallots and a crushed garlic clove to a little oil in the frying pan. Fry until translucent before adding a glass of red wine. Reduce until the sauce is about a third of its original volume. Who says sausages are fast food?

1 kg venison (any cut will do)
300 g pigeon breast, skinned
150 g breadcrumbs
150 ml deep red wine (anything dry, such as Bordeaux or rioja)
50 g chopped parsley
50 g minced onion
1 level teaspoon each of marjoram, cayenne and ground pepper
2 level teaspoons salt

1. First, sterilise all your equipment (see also page 32). Chill the meat and the grinder to as near to freezing as you can without making the meat solid. Allow roughly an hour or two for this.

2. Cut the meat into 5 mm cubes. Roughly grind all the meat and incorporate with the remaining ingredients in a bowl. For a more even mix, dissolve the salt in the wine. Grind again with the fine plate in place.

3. Stuff loosely into hog casings and then refrigerate overnight in a bowl covered in Clingfilm or a lidded plastic box before cooking.

An alternative is to stuff the into beef middles, then cook and slice (see offal sausage, page 50). The beef middle resembles an old sock when you get it out of the packet but gives a sausage 50 mm in diameter. I use beef middles for making black pudding and you do believe they will never be anything but thick-skinned and gelatinous on the inside because this is how they feel. However, once cooked the skin seems to contract in thickness and becomes the consistency of a black pudding skin.

One of the benefits of using these larger skins is that they do not need mechanical stuffers but can simply be filled with a spoon. Knot one end and then stuff the casing quite well, pushing down with the spoon. Then tie the other end and bake in the oven for 35 minutes (preheat to 180°C/Gas 4). The resulting sausage can be sliced diagonally to make a seriously lovely presentation.

Offal sausage

The origin of the word 'offal' comes from the early Dutch and thence to Middle English, and it means to throw away or refuse. It was the part of a butchered animal that ordinarily speaking, the rich people would not eat. However, poor people had no choice, and they became highly inventive in making the discarded internal organs very tasty indeed. So much so that many dishes found their way onto royal tables, and poems were written about some of them.

Of course we all know pâtés and sweetmeats, and their importance in continental cuisine, but the majority of UK offal, apart from maybe liver and onions and bacon ribs, steak and kidney, is used in sausages.

Black pudding

To make black pudding at home can be a somewhat off-putting process until you get used to it. Something about the smell of the blood caused me difficulty but having got used to it, the process really isn't that bad at all.

Maybe the easiest way to get started is to use a kit (available on the internet), which has all the seasoning and the blood – you simply need to add fat and pearl barley. In essence you mix the blood and seasoning in warm water (the kit even has salt already measured out), then add the fat, which is usually suet, but you can use back fat or other fats too. Following this you add the cooked pearl barley, which has been simmered until soft but not mushy. This is then poured into beef middle skins (of more below), which usually come with the kit, and link with firm knots before boiling for the prescribed time. I have to be honest and say the last thing I felt like was black pudding, having smelt it cooking, but after allowing it to cool and putting it into a sealed box in the fridge, a couple of days later it was sliced and eaten with enjoyment.

There are a number of ways to make black pudding and if you really cannot pluck up the courage to make your own, either from basic materials or a kit then you can still enjoy the intense flavour of black pudding by making your own black pudding sausage, with pieces of black pudding in it.

Beef middles

These are the large skins used for making black puddings. Although they look somewhat different to ordinary skins, don't be put off. They are packed in salt in the normal way, and need to be soaked. You do not use a stuffer, but either a funnel or a spoon. Funnels specifically designed for the purpose are available, but personally I have always found them to be a little fiddly.

The inside of the skins seem gelatinous and a little unusual, being almost furry. However, when cooked this disappears and you are left with a strong and thin skin. Obviously you will need to knot the end of the skin, but this should be backed up with butcher's twine that has been pre-soaked in water.

Every link should be twisted and tied off. Yes, in factories they link them more or less in the usual way, but in the kitchen a belt and braces approach is really beneficial, so link and tie off.

Cooking black pudding

Black pudding sets itself, which is a natural phenomenon of blood. When cooked, the liquid mush naturally forms a crumbly stuffing. One of the problems I have is the smell of the blood; it really puts me off eating black pudding, which I love so I make black pudding at a time when I do not wish to eat it, and freeze as soon as it is cold. This allows me time to get over the manufacture process, forget the off-putting experience and then enjoy my black pudding.

I also cook black pudding outside, which means the aroma (which really isn't that bad so don't be put off) isn't spread around the house.

Black pudding
Makes about 8 puddings

Let's be clear, you can no longer make black pudding from raw blood. It is now made using pelleted blood, or powdered blood that is obtainable from sausage making companies. You will also need 2 metres of beef middle casings.

500 g oatmeal
500 g barley
500 g pork fat
A little oil for frying
3 onions, diced
2 litres pigs' blood
25 g curing salt
2 teaspoons crushed black pepper
2 teaspoons fresh chopped coriander
2 teaspoons dried sage
2 teaspoons mace

1. Soak the oatmeal overnight according to the directions on the package and boil the barley for 30 minutes in salted water. Wrap in a tea towel to dry them both off as much as possible.

2. Dice the pork fat into 3 mm cubes, or as small as you wish. Some recipes call for suet, and if you replace the pork fat for suet, put the appropriate amount in the freezer and then grate it.

3. Lightly fry the onions in a large saucepan in a little oil until translucent, then add the oatmeal and barley. Add the pigs' blood, stirring all the time, and the remaining ingredients.

4. Wear gloves for the next stage, which is filling your casings and tying off at about 7 cm intervals. You can use a spoon, jug or funnel to do this; I do not recommend the special fillers on the market. Pop the pudding into boiling salted water for about 20 minutes (they will rise when cooked).

Using a kit

You can buy a black pudding kit with everything you need. Some of them come with suet, some with pearl barley and others with just a packet of spices and a packet of dried blood. Some come with skins and others don't, so make sure you check what you are getting for your money.

Using a kit is safe when it comes to the amounts of spices and salt, and you know for sure that the flavour will be more or less right. It can be very easy to make black pudding with a kit. Whether it is financially viable or not is another matter.

Black pudding sausage

This is simple to do: all you need is to make a basic pork sausage, as found in this book (page 32), but replace the bread portion with the same amount of black pudding. You should add half the salt at first, cook a small portion and then add extra salt to taste.

If you are going to make a black pudding sausage, use the freshest black pudding you can get – often the best thing to do is to buy direct from the manufacturer's outlet such as a local market, and you can get them still hot. Let the black pudding cool completely before adding it to the sausage meat, and then cool everything in the fridge before cooking or freezing.

Of course it is important to slice open the black pudding and scoop out the stuffing material before adding to the sausage meat, discarding the black pudding casing altogether.

Liver sausage
Makes about 4 large sausages

This is not so common in the UK as it used to be, but I have found that homemade liver sausage is far superior to anything you can buy. There are lots of variations on this recipe out there but I prefer this one, with a touch of garlic in the mix. Once cooked, it doesn't keep very well and therefore you need to eat it up within 3–4 days or freeze it. I always use fresh liver.

1 kg fresh pork liver
1.5 kg pork shoulder
2 teaspoons pepper
3 g allspice
1 teaspoon dried marjoram
250 ml iced water
1 onion, grated
2 garlic cloves, crushed under the flat of a knife and then chopped
25 g curing salt

1. Cut the liver into 5 cm pieces and bring to the boil in some water (don't overcook the liver). Allow to cool. Meanwhile, dice the pork shoulder into 2.5 cm cubes

2. Grind the liver and pork with the coarse plate and then repeat with the fine plate according to the manufacturer's instructions. This recipe calls for a very fine mix so if it isn't really fine, grind again. Remember, ancient recipes call for a lot of pounding.

3. Combine the spices, herbs and iced water. Mix with the meat, using your fingertips and thumbs to get the mix even. Finally, thoroughly combine the onion, garlic and curing salt with the meat.

4. Stuff into large pork casings, 36 mm in diameter, knot the ends well and simmer in water for 40 minutes. Check the internal temperature is a minimum of 75°C (167°F) for at least 20 minutes. Place in a bowl covered with Clingfilm or a plastic lidded box and keep in the fridge to serve cold.

Chicken liver sausage
Makes 6–8 large sausages

This version is almost a pâté in a skin, and very tasty it is too. You can vary the garlic content if you like, and double the amount of sage. I have seen recipes for this sausage using chicken, veal and turkey to make a light coloured version. The garlic needs to be ground as well as crushed to avoid any bitterness. You will need 28 mm diameter hog casings.

1 kg chicken livers (keep them very cool)
1 kg beef (any cut will do)
150 ml chilled red wine
20 g curing salt
1 teaspoon ground black pepper
4–6 garlic cloves, crushed and ground
25 g chopped fresh sage

1. Use a sharp knife to clean the livers of sinew and then wash in cold water.

2. Chill, cube and grind the beef with the medium plate, and then again with the fine plate with the chopped-up livers. Combine with all the other ingredients in a bowl to make a good paste.

3. Stuff into hog casings to make a taut sausage which can be boiled for about 30 minutes.

Haggis
Makes 1 haggis

This 'great chieftain o' the puddin-race' has to be included in a
sausage book. Thankfully you can make a really pleasing haggis
without having to use a sheep's pluck (the heart and lungs). One
recipe I have calls for you to boil the pluck in a large pan, leaving
the windpipe over the side of the pan, with a pot to catch the drips!
So, is this a sausage or a stew, or a meatloaf made of offal? Well,
with the idea that a sausage is in a skin, then it's a sausage. There
are many different recipes for haggis that would suit a modern
palette, especially in the making. You can vary the ingredients,
but the important ones are listed here. Use these quantities for
every kind of coarsely ground meat products you have.

500 g oatmeal
200 g chopped suet
4 large onions, diced
12 g curing salt
7 g cracked black pepper
20 g mixed herbs
2 teaspoons allspice
200 ml boiling stock

Casings
You can buy non-edible casings for haggis, or you can use Beef
Cap skins. They need to be tied off with butcher's twine, which
is quite important. Casings will need to be soaked, preferably
overnight.

The meat portion
If you can manage a sheep's pluck, all well and good! The thing
to do is to remove the windpipe, roughly cut the rest into
portions that will easily fit into a food processor and boil in a pan
for 2 hours. The portions are then coarsely ground. A pluck will
weigh around 2 kilos.

Most of us will struggle to get a pluck except by ordering one from the butcher's, and then my experience is they are not all that willing to get one because it is expensive. Abattoirs tend to send these straight off for animal feed, and consequently the action of holding one back is thought of as being a bit of a nuisance.

There are recipes out there that simply call for lamb's liver and oatmeal, still others that require a mixture of minced lamb, minced beef and oatmeal. This recipe attempts to get to the heart of the matter without using lungs with a combination of minced lamb, heart and liver with oatmeal, onion and spices.

You can make haggis from a number of other meats, keeping liver, heart and pork shoulder in equal proportions. You can get your butcher to clean the hearts for you and also to remove the sinews. Boil for about an hour on a slow simmer (add salt if you like) and then roughly grind, or use the food processor, reserving 200 ml of the stock. It is important that you do not cause the meat to form a fine paste: it should be roughly ground using the medium plate.

Allow the meat to cool and mix with all the dry ingredients in a bowl before adding the stock. Pack into casings and tie off. Each case will hold about 500–750 g of mix. Do not overstuff the casing because the contents will expand as the haggis is simmered in water for 3 hours.

This dish is traditionally served with neeps and tatties. Basically, potato and turnip mashed with a big knob of butter and richly peppered.

Baked haggis in a loaf tin
Makes 1 haggis

In making a haggis you are really making a kind of meatloaf that is held together in a skin, therefore making it a sausage. This is an important consideration when you come to think about the economics of haggis making. Sometimes it is just as well to bake the haggis in a loaf tin without a skin. Do the maths: the most expensive part of this recipe is the 'beef cap' skins you need for the sausage.

1 lamb's heart
250 g minced lamb
250 g lamb's liver
250 g suet
500 g oatmeal
2 large onions
1 teaspoon cayenne pepper
1 teaspoon cumin
1 teaspoon rosemary
1 teaspoon thyme
2 teaspoons salt

1. Remove the gristle and other 'non-meats' from the lamb's heart. Chop the muscle into small pieces and place in a pan with the other meats and simmer in just enough water to cover for an hour. Keep the cooking liquid but drain the meat and allow to cool.

2. Mince the meat with the large plate or roughly chop with the food processor. You don't want a paste, but you don't want chunks either.

3. In a bowl, combine all the dry ingredients and add the meat, mixing with your hands for a long time to ensure the salt is evenly distributed. Add the cooking stock, a little at a time, until you get a firm but moist dough-like sausage mixture. Stuff into beef middles (see also page 51) and tie off.

4. To cook the haggis it is best to stand a loaf tin in a little water in a heat proof dish and then bake at 200°C (Gas 6) for 1½ hours – don't let the water dry. If you have no skins, you can pile the mixture in a double layer of aluminium foil so it makes a fat haggis shape and then cook in the same way. You can also freeze it in a freezer bag or vacuum pack for up to a month if the meat hasn't already been frozen.

Och aye pie
Serves 4

We make what we call 'Och Aye Pie' with the materials left over from making haggis. This is a shepherd's pie with haggis meat added to it, the proportion is not important. The basic recipe is easy – you simply won't believe the effect of the haggis on the basic cottage pie.

4 small baking potatoes
A little butter for frying and mashing
1 large onion, finely chopped
500 g beef mince
500 g haggis (or whatever you have left over)
350 ml beef stock or water
Thickening (2 rounded teaspoons of cornflour mixed to a paste with
2 tablespoons cold water)
Salt and pepper
A little double cream

1. Bake four small potatoes at 190°C (Gas 5) for 35–40 minutes or until tender.

2. Meanwhile, sweat off the onion. Add the beef mince, 500g haggis and stock. Stir the thickening into the simmering mixture and season to taste.

3. Scoop out the cooked potato and return the skins to the oven to dry out completely.

4. Mash the potato with butter and cream. Layer up the pie by spreading the meat mixture in the base of an oven-proof dish, top with potato and bake for 20 mins in a moderate oven. Serve the potato skins on the side.

Fat bangers
Makes about 10 sausages

These sausages are higher in fat and salt than most of the recipes you will find in this book. Nonetheless, they are very tasty and will last for about a week in the fridge before cooking. It is a coarse sausage, but the use of pork loin means it has a delicate bite because there is less connective tissue in the sausage. Use hog skins, at 22–28 mm diameter.

300 g back fat
1 kg pork loin
150 g breadcrumbs
150 ml iced water
15 g salt
3 g white pepper
50 g fresh sage
50 g fresh thyme
3 g mace

1. Chop the fat to around 2 mm, then mince the pork loin with the medium grinder blade. Combine all the ingredients in a bowl before stuffing into the skins (link by twisting at about 7 cm).

2. Leave in the fridge overnight before cooking or freezing. Freeze in bags – I usually put a meal's worth in each bag.

Cumberland sausage
Makes 1 sausage

This is my take on the traditional sausage. You will have heard of
Cumberland rings, which is essentially a long coiled sausage that
isn't linked. This isn't particularly traditional, it is said that
miners came from Germany to Cumberland coalmines and
made their own sausage in this way as they did at home.

I have heard people say that sage is important, which is basically
completely wrong. You can use sage, but the main flavouring is
pepper and nutmeg. But you will find all kind of combinations
although the most important is a good amount of meat that is
coarsely ground only. I would use large hog skins for this sausage –
about 28 mm diameter – and this makes a sausage with a good bite.

600 g belly pork
500 g pork shoulder
100 g breadcrumbs (real bread is best in this recipe)
150 ml red wine or bitter beer (pale ale) or just plain water
15 g curing salt
7 g black pepper, loosely crushed
1 teaspoon nutmeg
1 g dried sage
1 g dried mace
A little oil for frying

1. Remove the skin from the belly pork and then cut the meat
into chunks that can be easily ground. Roughly grind the meat
and then add all the other ingredients. Fry a small amount in oil
to check the seasoning.

2. Place in the fridge while you prepare your skins and then stuff.
You can link, generously (page 35), or simply make a ring if you
prefer. Keep in the fridge overnight to firm up (in a bowl
covered in Clingfilm or a plastic lidded box) before cooking (fry
in a little oil for 20–25 minutes). Alternatively, freeze in freezer
bags or vacuum packs for about 3 months.

Gloucester sausage
Makes about 10 sausages

This is a different sausage in as much as it uses suet as the fat portion, and it is very savoury indeed. Over the years of making it I have cut down the amount of fat in the recipe, and I believe the amount in this recipe is perfect for both frying and using as a casserole sausage.

Many people think that sausages from the South West of the UK have apple in them, but this applies more to sausages from Somerset and Herefordshire. For this recipe use sheep casings at 18 mm diameter.

1 kg pork loin
200 g suet
225 g breadcrumbs
200 ml iced water (or try red wine for a really rich sausage – it seems to go well with the suet)
15 g curing salt
1 teaspoon cracked black pepper
2 teaspoons finely chopped sage
¼ teaspoon nutmeg

1. Cube and coarsely grind the meat. Freeze the suet and then grate into the meat in a bowl before mixing in all the other ingredients.

2. Regrind the mixture with a fine plate in the mixer or alternatively, whizz in the food processor until you have a fine paste.

3. Stuff into sheep skins and link at about 20 cm (see also page 35). Keep in the fridge overnight (under Clingfilm, foil or in a lidded plastic box) before cooking or freezing.

Hog's face
Makes 8–10 sausages

If you want a truly flavoursome sausage, try hog face meat – it is quite amazing. But you don't have to do the butchering yourself if you don't fancy it. Your butcher, if you are lucky enough to have a good one near you, will do it for you. This is the best meat for making pressed ham too. This makes a big fat sausage for breakfast, so use hog skins.

Add sage, thyme or any other garden herb, if you like. Some recipes call for the addition of lemon zest – I suppose to cut through the fat – but this is a very tasty sausage as it is.

1 kg hog face meat
200 g breadcrumbs
125 ml water
3 teaspoons salt
3 g pepper
25 g mustard powder
3 g mace

1. First, cool the face meat for a couple of hours and then mince with your hands, a powered grinder or the cutting blade of a food processor. Simply add all the other ingredients and then enough water to make a paste for stuffing. Add the water gradually – you will need to judge if you require more or less water.

2. Stuff into hog casings at 28 mm diameter (see also page 34). Keep in the fridge overnight (cover with Clingfilm, foil or store in a plastic lidded box) before cooking or freezing.

Irish sausage
Makes about 8 sausages

These sausages are often produced by Americans who frequently call for all kinds of flavourings they somehow believe to be Irish. It sometimes includes garlic but I saw one recipe asking for leek! Add more sage if you like a stronger flavour but start small – you can always add more later. Use 28 mm diameter hog casings.

1 kg pork shoulder
1 kg shin beef
250 g pork fat
250 g breadcrumbs
250 ml water
20 g curing salt
25 g chopped sage
3 g black pepper
2 g allspice
20 g curing salt

1. First, cool the meat for a couple of hours.

2. Cube and grind the meat before cutting the fat into 5 mm cubes. Add the breadcrumbs before combining the remaining ingredients. Check for flavour and seasoning – remember, this sausage is quite salty.

3. Stuff into pig casings (see also page 34) and leave overnight in the fridge (cover in Clingfilm, foil or store in a plastic lidded box) before cooking or freezing.

Lincolnshire
Makes 10–12 sausages

Lincolnshire sausages are fairly high-fat sausages flavoured with sage leaves, which not only gives them extra flavour, but also provides additional keeping qualities.

They are often flavoured with pepper – and lots of salt too. Of course the colour of Lincoln is Lincoln Green, which comes from sage.

Lincolnshire has a climate particularly suited to the growing of sage, though these days it is not farmed so much in the county. There is a standard list of ingredients that makes a Lincolnshire sausage, and the Lincolnshire Sausage Association tries to ensure it is adhered to. Sage is also used in a number of other Lincolnshire products, from Haslett (a pâté made from offal with sage) to Lincoln Pork Pies.

The meat is roughly minced once only. This is another defining characteristic of the Lincolnshire sausage, for many others are ground to a fine paste. Use 28 mm diameter hog skins.

500 g belly pork
1 kg pork shoulder
225 g breadcrumbs
20 g curing salt
2–3 teaspoons chopped sage leaves
3–5 g white pepper
200 g crushed ice or 200 ml iced water

1. First, remove the skin from the belly pork, but keep the fat content. Slice into easily minceable pieces.

2. Mince with the medium plate, then mix this straight away with all the other ingredients. Stuff into hog casings (see also page 34).

3. The sausages are best 24 hours later (refrigerate, covered), but will also freeze well. It is best to keep them for 24 hours before freezing, and if possible, store in vacuum-sealed bags.

Pork and apple
Makes 12–14 sausages

This is a favourite sausage and particularly liked in the South West of the UK, where Gloucester Old Spot pigs are let loose on the apple orchards to clear up the gleanings. Often these apples would be partially fermented, and the animals always slept well after a day's munching! Use 18 mm diameter sheep casings.

1 kg pork shoulder
150 g breadcrumbs or rusk
2 teaspoons salt
1 teaspoon ground black pepper
150 g diced apple (5 mm pieces)
150–200 ml apple juice or cider, iced

1. First, cool your grinding machine (see also page 33) and grind the meat using your medium plate before re-grinding with the fine plate. Alternatively, put the meat in a food processor and then work to a fine paste.

2. Carefully and thoroughly mix the dry ingredients, perhaps with a little of the liquid, to get a completely well mixed sausage. Then add the apple and the remainder of the liquid until you get an easily pliable mix.

3. Stuff into skins and link by twisting at about 12 cm (see also page 34).

4. Place in the fridge overnight (cover in Clingfilm or foil or store in a plastic lidded box) to firm up before cooking or freezing.

Poultry and game sausages

Chicken and turkey sausages contain less fat than pork or beef so are good if you are watching your fat intake. These days handling poultry needs careful attention due to pathogens such as salmonella. However, some very tasty sausages can be made with poultry.

Whereas the salt portion of these sausages is important for the preserving qualities, it is also important to get the flavour right. As with all the recipes in this book, test the seasoning by frying and tasting a small patty of the mixture before stuffing, adding more or less seasoning to your taste.

All the recipes in this section are good to freeze as soon as they are made but make sure you use poultry or game that has not been previously frozen.

Basic chicken sausage
Makes 15–18 sausages

Some people mistakenly call this 'boudin blanc' because it is white. But this isn't right at all, and traditionally boudin blanc was a very fatty sausage. Use mainly thigh or leg meat as it has more taste than breast. Use sheep or small hog casings 22–28 mm in diameter.

2 kg chicken meat (bones removed but leave the skin on)
1 small onion or half a larger one, finely chopped
1 garlic clove, grated
20 g curing salt
2 teaspoons caster sugar
1 level teaspoon mustard powder
½ teaspoon dried sage
1 teaspoon dried parsley or 1 tablespoon fresh chopped
200 g breadcrumbs
A little water

1. Chill, cube and finely mince the meat and place in a bowl. Add the onion and garlic then mix together well.

2. Put the salt, sugar and other seasonings in a small dish and combine well. Mix them into the meat, add the breadcrumbs with a little water to make a pliable mixture and massage for a minute to enhance the flavours.

3. Prepare the casings and the method of stuffing (see also page 34). Fill the casings evenly, linking at about 12 cm for sheep casings, 8 cm for hog casings (see also page 35).

4. Leave covered in the fridge for at least an hour before cooking or freezing.

Chicken and tarragon
Makes 15–18 sausages

There are many different types of tarragon, the best being French tarragon, which for the purposes of this sausage is the only one really used. Spanish tarragon is not so bad but do not bother with the Russian variety – it varies in flavour, and is quite unsuitable. Another alternative is sage, or a combination of sage and tarragon. Use sheep or small hog casings, 18 mm in diameter.

2 kg chicken thigh meat (leave the skin on)
20 g curing salt
2 garlic cloves, chopped
1 teaspoon mustard powder
1 teaspoon black pepper
2 tablespoons fresh tarragon, finely chopped
¼ teaspoon grated nutmeg
200 g breadcrumbs
A little water to make a smooth pliable paste

1. Chill, cube and finely mince the chicken then place in a mixing bowl. Add the salt and garlic and mix well.

2. Combine the seasonings, tarragon and nutmeg and add to the meat, mixing well with your hands. Add the breadcrumbs and a little water; mix to a pliable paste.

3. Prepare the casings and the method of stuffing and fill evenly, then link to 18 cm (see also pages 35).

4. Leave covered in the fridge to settle for at least 2 hours before cooking or freezing.

Chicken and sun-dried tomato
Makes 15–18 sausages

This is one of the made up sausages we have really enjoyed eating over the years, from experimentation with other recipes. You can also use this basic recipe with pork or beef, but it doesn't seem to work so well with lamb. Sheep casings (18 mm diameter) are best for this sausage. The sausages are fine served hot, but also brilliant cold.

2 kg chicken thigh meat (skin on)
100 g breadcrumbs
20 g curing salt
2 teaspoons caster sugar
80 g sun-dried tomatoes, drained if from a jar
1 tablespoon tomato purée mixed with 4 tablespoons water
2 garlic cloves, chopped
2 teaspoons ground black pepper
½ teaspoon ground cumin
3 tablespoons basil leaves, roughly torn

1. Cool, dice and mince the chicken then place in a mixing bowl and mix in the breadcrumbs, salt and sugar. Use the medium plate in the grinder, or roughly mince in the food processor.

2. Chop the tomatoes and place in a bowl. Pour over the tomato purée mixture. Add the tomato mixture and garlic to the meat and mix well.

3. Sprinkle over pepper, cumin and basil then mix in with your hands, massaging the flavours into the meat.

4. Place in the fridge for an hour before re-mincing with the fine plate or make a paste in the food processor. Prepare the casings and method of stuffing and fill with the meat mixture; link to around 18 cm (see also page 35).

5. Cover and leave to rest in the fridge for about 2 hours before cooking. Bake at 160°C (Gas 3) for about 20 minutes.

Turkey and cranberry
Makes 15–18 sausages

You can get turkey meat fairly cheaply at any time of year and this recipe makes a low-fat, low-cholesterol sausage that is quite inexpensive. Do not use any previously cooked meat in this sausage; the meat needs to be as fresh possible and preferably not hung.

Use 18 mm diameter sheep casings.

2 kg turkey meat
20 g curing salt
1 teaspoon white pepper
150 g breadcrumbs
4 tablespoons port
4 ice cubes
4 heaped tablespoons cranberry sauce

1. Chill, cube and mince the turkey using the medium plate in the grinder or roughly in the food processor, then place in a bowl.

2. Sprinkle over the salt and pepper. Add the breadcrumbs and port. Place the ice cubes in a tea towel, crush with a rolling pin and then sprinkle into the mixture. Mix well with your hands.

3. Add and combine the cranberry sauce, aiming to keep the cranberries in the sauce as whole as possible.

4. Prepare the casings and the stuffer; fill the casings evenly and link to 18 cm (see also page 34).

5. Cover and leave in the fridge for 2 hours before cooking or freeze in freezer bags or vacuum packs.

Duck and orange
Makes 15–18 sausages

This recipe was inspired by a visit to a hotel deep in the countryside, where I ate duck with orange sauce for the very first time. The acidity of the orange is the perfect counter to the fatty duck. Use 18 mm diameter sheep casings.

1 kg duck meat
1 kg pork loin
100 g breadcrumbs
20 g curing salt
1 level teaspoon ginger
Zest and juice of 1 large orange
100 ml orange juice
Pinch grated nutmeg
Pinch grated mace

1. Mince the duck and pork together with the medium plate or roughly in the food processor and place in a bowl. Sprinkle over the breadcrumbs and salt then mix together well with your hands.

2. Put all the other ingredients together in a small dish and stir to combine. Make holes in the meat with your fingertips and pour over the orange mixture. Massage it into the meat, adding a little more water to moisten, if necessary.

3. Prepare the casings and method of stuffing. Fill the casings with the meat mixture and link to 18 cm (see also page 34). Cover in Clingfilm or place in a plastic lidded box and allow to rest for about 2 hours in the fridge before cooking. Alternatively, freeze in freezer bags or vacuum packs.

Venison sausages
Makes about 12 sausages

Venison is a really healthy, lean meat. Some might say it's a little expensive for sausages, but in the country sometimes it comes your way and that's cool! The recipe is for 1 kg of venison meat because that's all I have ever made. It is very low-fat, and this can be a problem: fat has to be added, either by diluting the meat with belly pork, or by adding pieces of pork back fat. Personally, I prefer the former. Use 28 mm diameter hog casings.

Other seasonings may be added to vary this recipe. For example, ½ teaspoon juniper berries and rosemary instead of thyme, and port to replace the wine. As the flavour of the venison is so good, it's best to go for simple combinations.

1 kg venison meat
500 g belly pork (skin removed)
250 g streaky bacon, chopped
15 g curing salt
1 teaspoon ground black pepper
150 g breadcrumbs
½ teaspoon dried thyme
1 garlic clove, chopped
150 ml chilled red wine

1. Cool, dice and then mince the venison, pork and bacon together and place in a bowl. Use the medium plate on the grinder or roughly work in the food processor. Sprinkle over the seasoning and the breadcrumbs, then mix into the meat.

2. Add the thyme and garlic to the wine and stir well. Make holes in the meat with your fingertips and pour wine into them. Massage the mixture until all is combined.

3. Prepare the casings and the method of stuffing. Evenly fill the casings with the meat mixture and link to 18 cm (see also page 34).

4. Cover in Clingfilm or place in a plastic lidded box and allow to rest for 2 hours in the fridge before cooking. Or place in freezer bags or vacuum pack prior to freezing.

5. I find oven roasting in a greased roasting pan the best and gentlest method of cooking these sausages. Preheat the oven to 160°C (Gas 3) and cook for about 25–30 minutes.

Rabbit sausages
Makes about 10 sausages

Again, like venison, rabbit is really wonderful meat – healthy and wholesome. Where we live there are so many of them, and since they eat my vegetables, I feel it is only fair to return the compliment by eating them! Rabbit is a very lean meat, and therefore we treat it as though it were venison. Use 22 mm diameter hog casings for this recipe.

750 g rabbit meat
250 g streaky bacon
500 g belly pork
15 g curing salt
1 teaspoon white or black pepper
1 teaspoon mustard powder
¼ teaspoon dried thyme
150 ml dry white wine
100 g breadcrumbs
A little water, if necessary

1. Chill, dice and mince the meats together and place them in a bowl.

2. In a small dish, mix the salt, pepper, mustard powder and thyme together. Sprinkle over the meat and mix together well with your hands. Add the wine and mix into the meat. Sprinkle over the breadcrumbs and mix in (add a little water if the mixture is too dry).

3. Prepare the casings and method of stuffing. Fill the casings evenly with the meat mixture and link to 10 cm (see also page 35). Place on a tray, cover in Clingfilm or store in a plastic lidded box and refrigerate for 2–3 hours before cooking. Alternatively, place in freezer bags or vacuum pack prior to freezing.

4. These sausages are best cooked in a cassoulet, just like Toulouse Sausage, page 84, but they can be grilled or fried too.

Mixed game sausage
Makes about 12 sausages

This is the best Pigs in Blankets' sausage you can find anywhere! Wrap a rasher of streaky bacon around each sausage and bake until a rich brown at 180°C (Gas 4) for 25 minutes. Use 22 mm diameter hog casings.

500 g venison meat
300 g rabbit
300 g pheasant or duck meat
400 g belly pork
15 g curing salt
1 teaspoon ground black pepper
200 g breadcrumbs
5 juniper berries, crushed
150 ml red wine

1. Chill, dice and mince all the meats together and place in a bowl. Sprinkle over the salt and pepper and mix well with your hands.

2. Add the breadcrumbs and juniper berries; mix in. Pour over the wine and massage in with your hands.

3. Prepare the casings and method of stuffing. Evenly fill the casings with the meat mixture, linking at 10 cm. Cover in Clingfilm or place in a plastic lidded box and refrigerate for about 2 hours before cooking. Alternatively, freeze in freezer bags or vacuum pack.

Economical sausages

One of the advantages of making your own sausages is that you will enjoy better-quality food that is far more flavoursome too. Although the sausages in this section of the book are made from cheaper cuts you can rest assured that their contents are much healthier and a good deal tastier than many a cheap supermarket sausage.

Cheap-cut beef sausage
Makes about 8 sausages

You can use best steak for this recipe if you wish, but that would be a waste of money. It is best to use shin or skirt, or if you are really good with a small boning knife, oxtail, but this could be time-consuming. The idea behind this sausage is that it is cheap, and it is made cheaper by adding more breadcrumbs and water. Stuff them into 28 mm diameter hog casings.

These sausages can be smoked if necessary (see page 81), but they are supposed to be fried before serving. They also make brilliant cassoulet sausages, and particularly go well with a tomato sauce.

Augment them by adding a couple of crushed garlic cloves, or some paprika. In this way they are particularly lovely sliced and cooked on a pizza.

1 kg beef
200 g breadcrumbs
200 ml iced water
2 teaspoons salt
1 teaspoon cracked black pepper
3 g cayenne pepper
1 teaspoon dried sage
1 medium egg, beaten

1. Chop the beef into small chunks and then grind with the medium plate in the grinder. Mix in all the other ingredients except the egg before grinding again with the medium plate. Add the egg and mix completely to combine.

2. Stuff into hog casings and link by twisting at about 10 cm. Make the twists really firm, and knot the ends (see also page 51). Place in boiling water and cook for about 20 minutes. Drain and cool – you can freeze any not being used in freezer bags or vacuum packs for up to three months.

Oxford sausage
Makes 10–12 sausages

By rights this sausage should be in the 'Anyone can make sausages' chapter because the original recipes called for an egg or two to be beaten into the mixture and for the sausage to be dusted in flour and simply rolled into sausage shapes. So anyone can make an Oxford sausage.

In later years the addition of veal was something done in Oxford colleges, but it can be replaced by pork loin or chicken. Use sheep casings at 18 mm.

500 g pork shoulder
500 g veal
200 g pork back fat, diced into 2 mm pieces
200 g breadcrumbs
175 ml iced water
12 g curing salt
1 teaspoon cracked black pepper
½ teaspoon nutmeg
1 tablespoon dried sage

1. Grind the pork shoulder and veal together in the coarse plate and then mix in the remaining ingredients. Regrind with the fine plate or use the food processor to create a paste.

2. If you want to make the skinless version, keep the mixture in a bowl covered in Clingfilm overnight in the fridge for the flavours to develop, then fold in one medium egg and create sausage shapes that are then rolled in plain flour in the same way as the vegetarian sausages (page 28).

3. Otherwise, stuff into sheep skins and link at 12 cm (see also page 35). Keep overnight as before prior to cooking (these are best baked) or freeze them in freezer bags or vacuum packed.

Smoking sausage

There are a number of sausages that are smoked as a part of the preparation. The thing to remember when smoking sausage is not to use too heavy a wood: apple is perfect. There are two kinds of smoking, hot and cold.

Hot smoking

If you set a grill tray in a metal lidded box, put wood chips in the bottom and place the lot on a BBQ, the sausages will cook in a smoky atmosphere. They will be smoked, not in a preservation sense, but as far as flavour goes, this is simply delicious.

You can, of course, buy hot smokers, specially designed to allow the wood chips to burn slowly while at the same time not allowing it to escape so you can use them in the kitchen. Always use with caution, and be aware that many domestic smoke alarms these days are sensitive to heat.

The whole process gets very hot and you have to open the box to check the cooking of the sausage. Of course, as the sausage cooks, fat falls onto the wood and burns so it can be quite a trick to get it right.

Cold smoking

It is beyond the scope of this book to give a complete description of cold smoking, but there are a number of books on the subject on the market. Look out for ours coming soon! However, cold smoking can be achieved by buying a briquette burner (about £100 at the time of writing) that delivers cold smoke through a tube into a receptacle where the sausage is hung. The whole idea is to get the sausage in a smoky atmosphere that is not hot, and around 18°C (64°F) is acceptable.

Many people use old fridges for cold smoking. You hang your sausage inside so it doesn't touch the sides, although you must still disinfect it beforehand, and drill a hole through the side to accept the pipe. A few hours' smoking is usually all it takes.

Why smoke?

Apart from the incredible flavour, smoking also improves the keeping the smoked flavour qualities of the sausage, and is used with air-dried sausage. The smoked flavour goes particularly well with paprika, so chorizo is a good place to start. Smoking preserves in two ways: firstly the smoke is laden with aromatic oils that are poisonous to many bacteria and fungi. This combined with the particulate part of the smoke (the microscopic particles) forms a barrier to entry for many spoiling organisms.

The pellicle

The basic idea is to create a surface on which the smoke will adhere more easily. This is known as the pellicle. It is sometimes created by dipping the sausage in brine, then allowing it to dry prior to smoking.

Chapter 4
French sausages

There are many French sausages, which vary in nature from the dry south to the wetter west and northern sausages. On the whole they are highly spiced, or at least contain a lot of garlic, and are frequently used as ingredients in other dishes, such as the cassoulet.

Toulouse sausage
Makes about 15 sausages

This is one of my favourite sausage recipes. It is the key ingredient in a cassoulet but good in any sausage casserole. The meat should be very coarsely ground and the fat quite noticeable. You will need 28 mm diameter hog casings.

2 kg pork shoulder, cut into chunks
500 g belly pork
25 g curing salt
15 g brown sugar
150 ml chilled dry white wine
1 teaspoon white pepper
5 garlic cloves, chopped
3 g grated nutmeg

1. Cover and chill the meat for a couple of hours in the fridge and then cube. Coarsely grind the meat together and place in a bowl. Sprinkle over the salt and sugar; mix well. Add the wine, pepper, garlic and nutmeg. Massage well together with your hands to evenly distribute the flavour.

2. Fill the casings evenly, but do not overstuff them.

3. Link into individual sausages, about 12 cm in length, making the links as firm as you can (see also page 35). If you are going to cook the sausages in a cassoulet, fill and then knot before filling the next sausage. Alternatively you can tie off with butcher's twine.

4. Cover and leave overnight before cooking or freezing. The sausages can be frozen in freezer bags or vacuum packs for up to three months.

Figatellu garlic slicing sausage
Makes about 12 sausages

This is the one for garlic lovers! A cooked sausage that can be eaten hot, it is most usually reheated on pizza or in cassoulet or eaten cold. It is good with cheeses and salad.
You will need 2 m hog casings.

1.5 kg pork shoulder
500 g lamb's liver
20 g curing salt
5 garlic cloves, chopped
2 teaspoons sugar
3 g white pepper
2 g grated nutmeg
2 egg whites

1. Cover and chill the meat for a couple of hours, then cube and then finely grind it.

2. Combine all the ingredients in a mixing bowl and then massage into the meat with your hands. Do this for a few minutes so the meat is evenly flavoured with garlic.

3. Prepare the casings and your chosen method of stuffing. Stuff the casings with the meat mixture making sure there is as little air going through as possible to avoid air bubbles. Link the sausages into 15–18 cm lengths (see also page 35), then simmer for 15 minutes in hot water.

4. Oven bake at 160°C (Gas 3) for about 25 minutes.

Cervelas
Makes 12–15 sausages

This is an unusual French-style recipe that contains whole pistachios and brandy. In some recipes the nuts are replaced with truffles, and you can also use field mushrooms if you wish, but I prefer the pistachio. A mainstay of Lyonnaise cuisine, it is also very popular in Switzerland and further into central Eastern Europe. It is also popular in Germany, as it resembles a more cosmopolitan version of the Frankfurter.

Often these sausages are made from wild boar in the hunting season. Cervelas are boiling sausages and often served with mustard. You will need 28 mm diameter hog casings.

1.5 kg pork shoulder
500 g belly pork
20 g curing salt
2 teaspoons sugar
1 teaspoon white pepper
4 garlic cloves, finely chopped
½ teaspoon grated nutmeg
½ teaspoon dried thyme
150 ml chilled milk
3 tablespoons brandy
50 g pistachios

1. Cover and chill the meat for a couple of hours, then cube and finely grind before placing in a mixing bowl. Make holes in the meat with your fingertips then sprinkle over the dry ingredients except the pistachios.

2. Pour in the chilled milk and mix well with your hands. Add the brandy and massage into the meat, making sure it is evenly distributed.

3. Whizz the pistachios in the food processor, or place in a plastic bag, seal and bash with a rolling pin. Stir into the meat mixture.

4. Prepare the casings and your chosen way to stuff the sausages. Fill the casings evenly with the meat mixture. Link the sausages into about 12 cm lengths (see also page 35).

5. Place in a pan of simmering, salted water and cook for 20–25 minutes. You can serve either hot or cold.

Boudin blanc
Makes 4–6 sausages

This French sausage has a delicate flavour and was once almost all fat, though over the years it has had more meat introduced into it. The danger with boudin blanc is trying to add all sorts of flavours because it is a very mild sausage. Some people add a lot of salt, others add orange juice, but this peasant's sausage was never meant for modern paletes. Having tried a few recipes, some chicken-based, others based on veal and pork, the following is my favourite recipe, inspired by one originally found on the internet.

Do be careful not to store this sausage too long. It is low in salt, so treat it like fresh meat or freeze as soon as the sausages have cooled, following the poaching process. You will need 28 mm hog casings.

500 g pork shoulder
250 g pork back fat
A little oil for frying
1 onion, finely diced
50 g breadcrumbs (I much prefer breadcrumbs to rusk in this)
½ teaspoon thyme
2 teaspoons salt
3 g white pepper
300 ml milk
6 egg whites
1 whole onion

1. Cover and chill the pork for a couple of hours. Cube the pork and fat to make it easier to handle. Freeze the fat prior to grinding to increase its 'grindability'. Grind both with the coarse plate, then again with the fine plate.

2. Heat a little oil in a frying pan and cook the finely chopped onion very slowly over a gentleheat – don't let the pan get too hot, as you don't want any caramelisation.

3. In a bowl, combine the dry ingredients, then mix with the meat. Use about 100 ml of the milk and the eggs to shape into the sausage meat. The rest of the milk should be brought to the boil, then simmered with the whole onion in it.

4. Stuff the sausage meat into 28 mm hog casings and tie off firmly, double knotting the ends and using butcher's string to secure the twisted links. Add to the simmering milk and onion mix and poach for about 20–30 minutes (you might need more milk to cover during the cooking process).

5. Remove the sausages from the milk and allow them to cool (some people like to use iced water to quickly cool). When you are ready to eat, fry the sausages in a little oil to warm through and to brown the skins. Alternatively, the sausages can be placed in freezer bags or vacuum packs and frozen for up to three months.

Boudin noir
Makes about 8 sausages

Boudin noir is comparable to the British black pudding in that its main constituent is blood. However, boudin (which sounds like 'pudding' and both words have the same origin) does not have the variety of spices used in black pudding. Blood can be purchased in pelleted or powdered form over the internet. Note that in the UK it is no longer legal to use fresh blood for food manufacture. Use 28 mm hog casings.

1 kg pork shoulder
500 g pork back fat
500 ml pig's blood
3 medium baking apples
20 g curing salt
1 teaspoon white pepper
1 teaspoon finely chopped chives
1 teaspoon finely chopped coriander
4 garlic cloves, minced
200 g breadcrumbs

1. Cover and chill the meat, back fat and blood for a couple of hours. Cut the meat into small chunks and then mince with the coarse plate. Place in a large bowl.

2. Peel and slice the apples into 3 mm pieces and cut the back fat into 3 mm pieces too. Add to the bowl, together with the seasoning, herbs, minced garlic and breadcrumbs. Mix everything together well with your hands (you might wish to wear kitchen gloves for this).

3. Stuff the mixture into hog casing. This could be a messy process and is best done in a bowl of water, using a spoon to fill the casing. The end of the casing is knotted, and then the other end, knotted too, once full. Reinforce the knots and any links with butcher's twine. Boudin noir are often tied together at the end and sold as a U sausage.

4. Cook the sausage for 20 minutes in boiling water and check the interior reaches 75°C (167°F). Allow to cool and freeze (up to three months in freezer bags or vacuum packs) or use within a week (keep refrigerated). Great sliced and fried!

Peasant stew
Serves 8–12

Unashamedly carnivorous, this is really a kind of meaty soup which is mopped up with crusty bread. Traditionally, it contained a lot of offal, particularly kidney and heart, but this recipe is altered to suit modern tastes. In addition to the ingredients listed below you can also add ham shank or almost any other meat (bacon ribs are a favourite) and just stew the lot!

1 quartered rabbit
8 chicken pieces
A little oil for frying
8 Figatellu sausages (page 85)
200 g chopped onions
Half a savoy cabbage, shredded
10 whole garlic cloves, peeled
8 spring onion heads
About 500 g assorted mushrooms (any varieties, from ordinary button mushrooms to grizelles, porcini, which is often called 'the penny bun' where I live, and chanterelles)
Seasoning to taste
2–3 litres stock (vegetable is best because you will add flavours)
Crusty bread to serve

1. Wash the chicken and rabbit and then brown the rabbit portions in a little oil.

2. Place all the ingredients in a large pot, cover with stock and bring to the boil. Season and simmer for 3 hours, topping up with stock as necessary. Re-season to taste.

3. Simply pull out the bits you like to eat and pig out with lots of sauce and plenty of crusty bread!

Boudin blanc with wild mushrooms
Serves 2

The archetypal peasant dish, this can be recreated almost anywhere in Europe where woodland, fields, sunshine and rainfall make a wonderful spring and summer mix. However, do be careful when it comes to picking your own mushrooms. Sometimes what you think is edible is either mildly poisonous or simply full of bugs! Always be absolutely sure about mushrooms, or buy them from the shops. Better still, grow your own using one of the excellent kits available.

20 g butter
1 red onion, finely chopped
1 garlic clove, chopped
100 g wild mushrooms, chopped if large
A little oil for frying
8 x 1 cm slices boudin blanc (page 88)
100 ml cheap dry white wine
Salt and pepper to taste
1 tablespoon fresh chopped parsley
80 ml double cream

1. Melt the butter in a large frying pan and soften the onion over a low heat.

2. Add the garlic and wild mushrooms and stir well. Cook over a low heat for 5 minutes until the juices from the mushrooms begin to run. Meanwhile, fry or grill the boudin blanc.

3. Stir in the wine and season with salt and pepper. Raise the heat slightly to a simmer and stir well before stirring in the parsley and cream. To serve, place the boudin blanc on serving plates and pour over the mushroom mixture.

Didot de Savoie
Makes 10–12 sausages

This is produced in the deep south of France, and has Italian ancestry borne out in the fact that the cereal portion is usually polenta, but our version, also traditional, contains cabbage and breadcrumbs. Sometimes made from smoked meat, the sausages themselves are not smoked, but the meat is. Use 22 mm diameter hog casings

1.5 kg pork loin
125 g pork back fat
250 g cabbage, boiled, drained and shredded
200 g breadcrumbs
4 garlic cloves
3 g white pepper
15 g curing salt
100 ml white wine

1. The meat is covered and chilled for a couple of hours while the cabbage is cooled and draining. Once cooled to room temperature, shred the cabbage and place it in the fridge to chill further.

2. Cube the back fat as small as possible, 2 mm if you can. Cut the pork into managable pieces and then grind finely. Actually I tend to use the food processor for a fine paste. Add all the other ingredients and mix well.

3. Stuff into hog casings and link at 12 cm (see also page 35). These sausages can be cooked in a number of ways, from baking to frying. You can also freeze them in freezer bags or vacuum packs for up to three months.

Andouillette sausage
Makes 8–10 sausages

This sausage is a wonderful test of the sausage maker's art. You needn't grind anything, it's all cut. It is said to have been invented for a banquet for a French king in AD 900, just before they invaded the Champagne region. Some regions of France have their own versions containing veal as well as pork. For this recipe you will need 28 mm diameter hog casings.

1 kg pork loin
500 g tripe
1 medium onion
3 garlic cloves, crushed
1 tablespoon each of parsley, sage and thyme
15 g curing salt
3 g white pepper
150 ml dry white wine
Vegetable stock or water (see method)

1. Cover and chill the meat and tripe in the fridge for a couple of hours, then beat the pork flat, which also tenderises it. To do this, wrap in Clingfilm and then a tea towel before bashing away with a rolling pin. Roll this flattened meat and slice as finely as you can. If you can manage 2 mm strips, that is best – use a very sharp knife and just be careful! Chop the tripe into as small pieces as you can.

2. Shred the onion as finely as possible and then finely chop the garlic and herbs. Mix in a bowl with the meat, tripe, seasoning and wine and then manually stuff the sausage mixture into large hog casings, which are linked and then tied with butcher's twine to reinforce the link (see also page 51).

3. The sausages are then boiled for 25 minutes in enough stock or water to cover until cooked. Allow to cool and then fry or they can be grilled or eaten cold. Traditionally, the liquor the sausages are boiled in is turned to gel with aspic to preserve the sausage.

Chapter 5

German sausages

If you like sausages then you really need to go to Germany, because it is truly the home of sausage, partly because of the number of pigs the Germans once kept, but also because the working people traditionally provided the best food for the upper classes, and all they had left was made into sausage. This was good news for the peasantry because in times of need, sausages were more easily available and longer lasting than the more genteel cuts of meat.

Bratwurst-style sausages
Makes 12–15 sausages

Traditionally made with a combination of pork and veal, this version uses all minced pork. This spice and herb mix is to our taste so you may wish to try smaller amounts at first and taste test with a little patty of meat, building up the spices to suit you. Use 28 mm diameter hog casings.

2.5 kg pork shoulder
25 g curing salt
½ level teaspoon grated mace
½ level teaspoon grated nutmeg
1 teaspoon ground allspice
1 teaspoon white pepper
1 level teaspoon dried marjoram
1 rounded teaspoon dried parsley
1 level teaspoon celery seeds
250 ml iced water

1. Chill the meat for a couple of hours, then dice and grind it with the medium plate in a grinder, or roughly mince in a food processor. Place the meat in a large mixing bowl and push holes into it across the whole surface with your fingertips.

2. Put all the other ingredients except for the water in a small bowl and stir well to combine. Sprinkle this mixture evenly over the meat along with the iced water. Massage in well with your hands to enhance the flavours.

3. Link the sausages to 12 cm (see also page 35). Transfer to a bowl and cover in Clingfilm or place in a plastic lidded box. Leave covered in the fridge for at least 2 hours before cooking. The sausages can be fried, grilled or oven baked.

Nürnberger bratwurst
Makes 6–8 sausages

This recipe originates from the south of Germany and is a mixture of beef and belly pork. It is from the Wesch family, who came to the UK from Germany early in the 1900s to set up a sausage skin company that is still very active today. Use 18mm diameter sheep casings.

1 kg belly pork
300 g shin beef
12 g curing salt
3 g white pepper
1 g mace
¼ teaspoon nutmeg
1.5 g marjoram
Vegetable stock (see method)

1. Chill the meat for a couple of hours, then cube and grind it through the medium plate on the grinder.

2. In a large bowl mix together the remaining ingredients and grind again with the same plate. Stuff the sausage meat into sheep casings and link at about 20 cm (see also page 35).

3. The sausages are cooked by simmering in enough stock to cover until the insides reach 75°C (167°F) for 10 minutes.

Bierwurst
Makes about 12 sausages

A hot smoked slicing sausage that is eaten cold. The recipe calls for a lot of meat as it does make a lot of sausage. However, the word 'bierwurst' means beer sausage, and as such, you do need a lot of it to soak up all that alcohol! Use ox runners (50–75 mm wide) for the casings. At first glance they seem quite tough but when cooked they will shrink and resemble the skin on a black pudding.

2 kg beef shin or skirt, cut into chunks
2.5 kg pork shoulder, cut into chunks
½ –1 level tablespoon ground black pepper
1 level tablespoon mustard seeds
40 g curing salt
2 garlic cloves
350–400 ml iced water

1. Cover and chill the two meats for a couple of hours. Grind together until finely minced and place in a mixing bowl. This is best done by grinding with the medium plate and then again with the fine plate.

2. Sprinkle over the spices, salt and garlic, then massage well into the meat with your hands. Add sufficient iced water to make a pliant mixture – it should run easily through the fingertips.

3. Prepare the casings and your chosen method of stuffing (see also page 34). You need to soak the ox runners in cool water for a few hours. These casings can be stuffed with a spoon. Tie off the lengths at about 30 cm and use butcher's twine to reinforce the link. Transfer to a bowl and cover in Clingfilm or place in a plastic lidded box and refrigerate overnight. The sausages can be oven-baked, fried or grilled.

Liverwurst
Makes about 12 sausages

A tasty sausage that is quite similar in flavour to a good pork pâté. Use hog casings at 28 mm diameter.

1 kg pork liver, sliced
1.5 kg pork shoulder, chopped
200 ml iced water
1 medium onion, very finely chopped
20 g curing salt
½–1 level teaspoon dried sage
1 level teaspoon marjoram

1. Gently simmer the liver in sufficient water to just cover for a few minutes until it changes colour but is still very tender. Mince the pork and liver together until very smooth. If grinding in the mincer use the medium plate first, then the fine plate, mincing again to create a fine paste. Place in a bowl.

2. Add the iced water, onion, salt and herbs and mix together well, massaging the flavours into the meat with your hands.
Prepare the casings and your chosen method of stuffing. Stuff the casings well with the sausage meat mixture, making sure there are no air pockets. Link the sausages at 12 cm intervals (see also page 35).

3. Boil in simmering water for about 15 minutes. When cooked, leave to cool and serve cold in slices. You can also freeze the liverwurst as soon as it is cool enough to go in the freezer (it will freeze for up to 3 months) or vacuum pack and store in the fridge for up to 5 days.

Rookworst
Makes about 12 sausages

This sausage is based on a Dutch and Flemish recipe, which in its turn is based on the Bologna sausage that influenced many of the world's sausages. The name suggests it should be smoked but if you wish it can be oven-baked instead. Originally this was a smoked sausage but the majority on sale in shops have simply had smoke flavoured additives; the smoked paprika gives it a smoky flavour. They are tied off at about 60 cm long, folded in a 'U' shape and often tied at the ends. Use hog casings at 28 mm diameter.

2 kg pork shoulder
20 g curing salt
7 g ground black pepper
1 rounded tablespoon smoked paprika (more if you like!)
½ teaspoon dried marjoram
½ teaspoon fennel seeds
100 ml brandy

1. Cool the meat for a couple of hours, then dice and mince it as finely as possible. Transfer to a large bowl.

2. Combine all the seasonings in a small dish. Make holes in the meat with your fingertips and sprinkle the seasoning evenly over the surface. Rub in well before adding the brandy. Massage the meat so that everything is well incorporated.

3. Prepare the casings and your chosen method of stuffing then fill with the sausage meat mixture. Link the sausages and then form into a 'U', as is traditional with Rookworst if you wish. Cover and leave in the fridge for 3 hours, then cook the sausages. Place on a greased roasting tin and bake in the oven (160°C/Gas 3) for 45 minutes.

Frankfurters
Makes 12–15 sausages

These are the archetypal hot dog sausages found mostly in America, or in brine kept in jars. They are simple to make at home, and much tastier than the shop-bought versions.

You will notice that the majority of Frankfurters are straight sausages, but the ones in this recipe are not. The reason for this is the straight ones are stuffed into manmade skins. Use 22 mm diameter hog casings – you will need about 2 m.

1 kg lean pork, cubed
1 kg lean beef, cubed
250 g pork fat, cubed
2 teaspoons finely ground coriander
½ teaspoon dried marjoram
½ teaspoon ground mace
½ teaspoon ground mustard seeds
2 teaspoons sweet paprika
1 teaspoons finely ground white pepper
2 teaspoons sugar
20 g curing salt
200 ml milk
1 large onion, very finely minced
12 garlic cloves, crushed
2 medium eggs

1. Chill the meat and fat for a couple of hours (the fat needs to be really chilled or else it smears). Cube and very finely mince both using the medium plate on the grinder and then the fine plate, or in the food processor until you have a fine paste. Keep the meat covered in the fridge while you prepare the remaining ingredients.

2. In a bowl make a purée of the dry ingredients with a little of the milk. Add the onion, garlic cloves and eggs with the rest of the milk and then combine everything with the stuffing until it is evenly mixed. Cover and place the bowl in the coldest part of the fridge overnight for the flavours to develop.

3. Stuff the sausage mixture into sheep skins and link at about 20 cm (see also page 35). Place in boiling water and then simmer for 20 minutes. The sausages are then cooked before they are served in the traditional way, with boiled onions and cabbage and Mustard sauce (page 161).

Wiener
Makes about 12 sausages

The traditional hot dog sausage, it can be made with or without paprika. This sausage is the one that crossed the Atlantic and became world famous! Use thin hog skins at about 22 mm diameter.

1 kg pork shoulder
1 kg beef shoulder or chuck
2 teaspoons paprika (optional)
1 teaspoon English mustard powder
25 g curing salt
20 g sugar or honey (I use 3 big dollops)
1 teaspoon powdered black pepper
1 teaspoon coriander powder
5 garlic cloves, crushed
3 g ground mace
175 ml iced water

1. Chill the meat for a couple of hours, then cube and grind it twice, once with the medium plate and again with the fine plate. Mix with all the other ingredients except for the iced water in a large bowl.

2. To make the sausage as authentic as possible, it needs to be very finely ground. This is best achieved in a food processor, adding the meat in small amounts (a cupful at a time) with small amounts of water until everything is completely combined.

3. The sausages are cooked by boiling for 10 minutes. This is not enough to completely cook them but they can then be cooled and frozen. Finish off under the grill for about 10 minutes.

4. You can freeze the sausages in freezer bags or vacuum pack. They can be stored in the freezer for up to 3 months.

The best hot dog in the world!
Makes enough for about 20 dogs

The only way to truly enjoy Wieners is in a freshly baked and crusty roll, with onions piled on top, and plenty of sauerkraut as a base.

You can make the most sublime sauerkraut by shredding cabbage. Simply rinse, pat dry and weigh the cabbage (use a weight or a piece of wood for this). For each kilo of cabbage, use 15 g sea salt. In a large bowl mix the salt and cabbage together and with a squeezing action, rub the salt into the cabbage. The cabbage will wilt and you will then see a liquid that is salty.

Now press the cabbage down with your fists, cover with a plate and weigh down. You can keep it in the fridge for up to a month and have perfect sauerkraut to hand. Store in sterilised Kilner jars or in the pot in which it was originally made as they do in Germany and Holland.

Knockwurst
Makes about 12 sausages

For a German sausage this one has a bit of a kick! It makes a great snacking sausage. Use 28 mm hog skins.

1.25 kg shin beef
750 g pork shoulder
30 g curing salt
2 teaspoons ground black pepper
5 garlic cloves, crushed
3 g allspice
1 teaspoon mace
1 teaspoon coriander
7 g paprika
175 ml iced water

1. Chill the meat for a couple of hours, then cube before grinding with the medium plate of the grinder.

2. Mix the meat with the remaining ingredients and grind again with the fine plate, then repeat again. You need a very fine paste. Stuff into hog skins at 28 mm diameter and link at 10 cm intervals (see also page 35).

3. These sausages are often smoked, but I tend to hot smoke them myself so they are cooked at the same time. Alternatively they can be boiled for 15–20 minutes or bake on a greased baking tray for 20–30 minutes in a preheated oven (180°C/Gas 4).

Chapter 6

Southern European sausages

Spain and Italy have a history of making great sausages, including some of the earliest recipes still in frequent use today, such as the Lucanian sausage and Mortadella. In Italy people still use thumb stuffers, which are great for making salami on beef runners. Simply load the skin onto the end of the funnel and then use your thumbs to force the stuffing mixture into the skin.

Spanish sausage – Chorizo

One of the archetypal sausage recipes that people always want to make, chorizo has become something of a rite of passage for the home sausage maker. It is an air-dried sausage and as such not so easy to complete in the wet UK climate. To make this sausage you need a clean, reliably uniform space that is not too hot, nor too dry, too moist or too cold.

The way chorizo works is to combine many preserving functions into one sausage to make it safe. It has to be said this sausage is not cooked and consequently you need to get the whole thing right, otherwise you will have a product that is either inedible or dangerous.

Salting

First of all, the chorizo is quite heavily salted, using curing salt – don't attempt to use any other form of salt – it must have saltpetre as part of the salt to be sure to deal with botulinum, the most acutely lethal toxin known.

Microbial starter (fermented starter)

A culture of microbes in the sausage is an important element in the development of this particular sausage. It is often sold as a Bessastart starter for chorizo, but if you ask for chorizo culture, you will get the right stuff. These microbes live off the meat sugars and give off lactic acid. They give the sausage a bitter taste and also a degree of bacterial safety because the acid kills the bacteria.

You can also ferment chorizo by using a yoghurt culture, which is essentially live yoghurt added to the mixture, and it does work.

It is important to recognise that some chorizo are not fermented; they get the tang by the addition of vinegar to the mixture. Such chorizo are always cooked prior to eating, though.

In order to ferment a chorizo, you need a drying cabinet or safe space. The temperature should be around 20–22°C (68–71°F) in order to get the starter working, and then for drying at about 12°C (53°F), and the relative humidity should be around 75 per cent. Serious sausage makers have their own drying cabinets, some of these costing many thousands of pounds. Still others use clean and sometimes adapted old fridges.

Spices
The garlic, paprika and other ingredients in chorizo provide some important protection from spoiling bacteria.

Air-drying
The sausage is hung for long enough to ensure a loss of about 30 per cent of its weight by evaporation. This, along with the osmotic pressure imputed in the sausage from the salt and the spices, means the micro environment is unsuitable for microbial growth in the sausage. Where water is not available, there is no life. Osmotic pressure, incidentally, is the way highly concentrated salty substances pull water to them, dissolving them in what is often a violent process, and explains why sea water dries our skin.

Smoking
Some chorizo are smoked, others are not. Smoking increases the osmotic pressure in the sausage; and it provides complex aromatic molecules that are poisonous to bacteria.

Lots of recipes

There are hundreds of recipes for chorizo out there and it must be said that clearly many of them haven't been made by their originators! Personally, I would avoid any recipe that doesn't have curing salt in it as a basic minimum. However, in Spain there are dozens of recipes for chorizo, almost as many as there are villages. Some of them produce sausages that are only semi-dried and then oven-baked, or sliced and cooked for toppings, or cooked in a cassoulet.

Then there are various recipes for Spanish sausages in the diaspora, particularly in Mexico. What we call paprika is termed 'pimentón' in Spain and comes from Mexico. The flavours of the Mexican pimentón are much hotter than the sweeter Hungarian that we are more accustomed to in the UK. So the Spanish sausage is somewhat different depending on the region of its origin, unlike the British banger, which is much the same the world over!

Starter cultures

Starter cutures are mixtures of bacteria that are added to the sausage meat. They are alive in the sausage and convert the meat sugars to lactic acid, which is what gives the sausage a tangy flavour. The acidity also helps to preserve the sausage. If the sausage is also smoked, this helps to preserve it too.

Chorizo
Makes 12–15 sausages

Easy to make and delicious. Note no extra fat is added to this
sausage. You will need hog skins at 28 mm diameter.

1 kg lean pork
1 kg belly pork
3 garlic cloves, crushed
2 teaspons dried chilli flakes
25 ml cider vinegar
4 tablespoons sweet Spanish paprika
25 g curing salt
3 teaspoons dried oregano
2 teaspoons freshly ground black pepper

1. First, cover and chill the meat for a couple of hours, then cube
and roughly grind it using the medium plate on the grinder.
Transfer to a large bowl.

2. Add all the remaining ingredients and mix together well.
Cover and leave in the fridge for 24 hours, then stuff the sausage
meat into the skins, linking at 7.5 cm (see also page 35).

3. Hang the sausages in a clean space for three weeks prior to
cooking or freezing. This allows water to evaporate from them,
increasing the flavour and also making it harder for microbes to
live in them. They are not to be eaten without thorough cooking.
Serve sliced on a pizza, in a cassoulet or individually. Once
cooked, they can also be eaten cold.

4. You can also freeze the sausages in freezer bags for up to three
months.

Fermented chorizo
Makes 4–6 sausages

This is a fairly simple chorizo, which is fermented. The main flavour comes from the paprika but the garlic and pepper give secondary flavours to create quite a complex effect. A fermented sausage is not quite like a fermented beer or a loaf of bread, the microbes used are different. They grow on the sugar in the sausage, releasing lactic acid which is poisonous to microbes and gives the sausage a certain tanginess. Chilled red wine prevents the sausage meat from warming in the preparation process. Use 28 mm diameter hog skins.

2 kg pork shoulder
250 g pork back fat
1 g starter culture
About 4 tablespoons warm water
50 g sweet paprika
2 teaspoons crushed garlic
1 teaspoon ground black pepper
25 g curing salt
150 ml chilled red wine
3 g glucose

1. Cover and chill the pork and back fat for a couple of hours, then dice and roughly grind with the medium plate in the grinder. Then return to the fridge for about an hour. Dice the back fat into 4–6 mm pieces.

2. Add the starter culture to about 4 tablespoons warm water. Mix all the ingredients and then re-mix with the starter liquid. It doesn't look as though it is growing in the water but it really is!

3. Transfer the pork, starter culture mix and the remaining ingredients to a large bowl and completely combine. Stuff into hog skins, linking at around 30 cm (see also page 35).

4. Cover the sausage and keep warm for 24 hours at room temperature before hanging for about a month in relative humidity of 75 per cent or less, and a temperature of around 12°C (54°F)

5. Once correctly fermented Chorizo doesn't have to be frozen but you can keep it in the freezer in food bags for up to three months. Alternatively, store in the fridge in a vacuum bag to keep it free of contaminants for up to a month.

6. Chorizo is eaten raw and can be sliced onto pizza or used in stews and cassoulet.

For bigger chorizo ...
To make a bigger chorizo sausage, use 40 mm diameter ox runner skins and stuff with a spoon. You will need to double up the original quantities and you could add some other ingredients too, including:

2 teaspoons fennel seeds
2 teaspoons oregano
2 teaspoons cumin
1 teaspoon chilli powder or chilli flakes

The drying of ox runners is slightly different in as much as the sausage is thicker, and consequently the centre should be really firmly cured. If in doubt, cook the sausage before eating.

Is your chorizo working well?
There are a number of checks you can do to make sure your chorizo is fermenting properly, losing water evenly and not being contaminated.

Acidity
On the whole the acidity of the sausage, as measured on the pH scale, should start at around pH 7. You can use a pH strip to test this. As the sausage ferments and the starter microbes work in the acidity will increase (and therefore the pH number should

decrease) so by the month's end it should be around pH5 (the stronger the acid, the lower the number).

Weight

The sausage should lose weight through the evaporation of water. You will need to weigh it several times during the fermenting process, first at the beginning after the 24-hour incubation period and then when you think it is done, possibly again, some days later. You are looking to see that the weight of the sausage has reduced by at least 30 per cent as it has dried out. So, for example, a sausage starting out at, say 1 kg, should be ready when it weighs about 700 g.

Watch out for strange smells, blackness, oozings and very soft sausages. These are all signs of contamination. The sausage should resemble shop-bought chorizo: firm, sweet-smelling and uniformly coloured.

Look out for mould

Depending on the starter culture you use, the sausage should bloom and will usually have a white-ish coating. Any furring can be wiped away with a piece of kitchen roll soaked in vinegar. Discard any sausages that are black or smelly, oozing and/or unusually soft, or have any other striking unusual colour on the surface.

Pets and children

It is best if you can keep the sausage in a place to which children cannot gain access, and where you can closely monitor the progress of the sausage. The sausage is potentially dangerous until it is finished and shown to be safe. Make sure it is stored safely away from pets and other creatures such as rats and mice too.

A really important point is flies – they don't care a jot about salt, so be sure to keep the developing sausages free from flying insects.

Pork and chorizo
Makes about 8 sausages

This is a good recipe for those who do not feel confident in making their own chorizo but would still like to make a start. It is a bit like a black pudding sausage in as much as you can incorporate some chorizo into an ordinary sausage to make a completely different product. Use hog skins at 28 mm diameter.

220 g chorizo
1 kg pork loin
50 g breadcrumbs
75 ml iced water
2 teaspoons paprika
1 teaspoon salt

1. First, peel the chorizo with a knife so that you do not end up with skin in your sausage.

2. Cover and chill the meat for a couple of hours before dicing and grinding it. Grind twice, once with the medium plate and then again with the fine. Alternatively, make a paste of the meat in the food processor. Transfer to a large bowl.

3. Chop the chorizo as small as possible and add this to the meat with the remaining ingredients. Mix well to combine. Stuff the sausage meat into the skins and link at 12 cm intervals (see also page 35).

4. The sausages should be baked in a preheated oven set to 160°C (Gas 3) for 30 minutes. They can be eaten hot or cold.

How to cook with chorizo

Of course it is great sliced on pizza, but the majority of chorizo are used in stews. It is basically the Spanish equivalent of the French Toulouse sausage.

Chickpea and chorizo stew
Serves 4

A quick and easy supper dish that is great when you are extremely hungry and want something cooked in minutes.

750 g new potatoes, scrubbed but leave on the skins
A little oil for frying
1 medium onion, chopped
1 red pepper, deseeded and chopped
2 garlic cloves, chopped
1 tablespoon honey
200 g chorizo, skin removed and diced
1 level teaspoon paprika
400 g can chopped tomatoes
450 g can chickpeas, drained
Seasoning to taste

1. Put the potatoes in a saucepan and add sufficient hot salted water to just cover. Boil until just tender and drain.

2. Heat the oil in a large frying pan and fry the onion, pepper and garlic until softened. Stir in the honey and chorizo and sprinkle over the paprika. Reduce the heat and let the flavours cook together for 4–5 minutes, occasionally stirring.

3. Add the potatoes and stir to combine before adding the tomatoes and chickpeas. Check for seasoning and cook at a slow simmer for about five minutes then serve in big bowls.

Italian sausages

Chilli sausage
Makes 10–12 sausages

This sausage is all about getting the chilli just right. At times it is something of a fine art, not making an overpowering sausage, and consequently, this one is a good starting point. It is always a good idea to taste your sausage meat before stuffing, particularly with spiced sausages, so cook a small portion to get an idea of the heat and the seasoning. Use 18 mm diameter sheep skins.

Habanero chillies are hot, short and green when unripe and red when ripe. Handle chillies of all kinds with care: always wear plastic gloves and do not rub your eyes.

2 habanero chillies, deseeded
1 kg pork shoulder
100 g breadcrumbs
15 g salt
3 g black pepper
3 g paprika
2 medium onions, finely chopped
2–4 garlic cloves, minced
150 ml iced water (or substitute red wine)
20 ml red wine vinegar

1. Carefully mince the chillies and set aside. Cover and chill the meat for a couple of hours before dicing and mincing to a fine paste. Grind twice with the grinder, using medium and fine plates, or create a paste in the food processor. Transfer to a bowl and add all the dry ingredients.

2. Carefully combine the onions, garlic and chillies into the meat mix, cover and leave overnight in the fridge for the flavours to infuse. Make to a stuffing paste by adding the iced water and red wine vinegar the following day. Stuff and link at 18 cm intervals (see also pages 34-35).

3. Bake in a preheated oven (180°C/Gas 4) for 25 minutes or freeze in freezer bags for up to three months.

Mortadella
Makes 6 sausages

An Italian sausage in part at least derived from the Lucanian sausage of Roman times. More than any other sausage, the Mortadella has evolved into a whole raft of sausages, possibly because it was used as a staple food at the time of the great explorations, taken around the world on conquest. Settlers then created their own versions. Baloney, eaten throughout the Americas, was one such sausage and considered inferior to the original, leading to the saying 'a load of baloney' meaning something untrue or useless.

Originally a veal sausage, it is now more frequently made from pork. Use an ox middle casing to give a sausage about 65 mm in diameter when filled.

2 kg pork shoulder
150 g pork back fat
200 ml chilled red wine
200 ml iced water
25 g curing salt
3 g ground coriander
1 g ground cinnamon
3 g mace
4 garlic cloves, crushed
3 g fennel seeds
200 g Parmesan cheese, grated

1. Cover and cool the meat and fat for a couple of hours. Dice the fat into large (5 mm) chunks. Set the fat to one side, and do not mix with the ingredients at this stage.

2. Roughly grind the meat, transfer and mix in all the other ingredients apart from the fat. Cover and return to the fridge for an hour before re-grinding or blitzing in the food processor to create a smooth paste. Add the fat and mix well.

3. Soak the casings in three changes of water over an hour. Tie one end and stuff with a spoon, linking with a twist at 30 cm and reinforce the link with butcher's twine (see also page 51).

A little history ...

The original sausage was wrapped in caul fat and rolled as a sausage. The same result can be achieved using Clingfilm to make the shape. Just follow these instructions:

Use only half the Parmesan cheese, and replace with three eggs. Roll into a sausage about 7cm round, wrap in Clingfilm and set in the fridge overnight. Remove the Clingfilm and carefully place in a preheated oven at 150°C (Gas 2) for three hours.

Cooking

The cooking varies (different recipes call for different methods of cooking) but I tend to bake the mortadella for about three hours in a low oven preheated to 150°C (Gas 2), making sure the centre has reached at least 75°C (167°F) with a probe thermometer.

Allow the sausage to cool before eating or freezing. It can be frozen in freezer bags for up to three months.

Lucanian sausage
Makes about 12 sausages

This is a Roman sausage, possibly not the earliest sausage in the world but at around 2,000 years old, it's not bad at all. It contains fish sauce, which was essentially fermented fish bits and pieces that rotted down with a lot of salt to form a clear golden liquid called garum. This is no longer used in Italy, but there are some cultures such as Thai fish sauce which create a pretty reasonable substitute.

The Lucanian sausage was part of the basic daily allowance for Roman legions fighting their way around the Empire and consequently may well have been the first meat of this kind to be eaten in many parts, including Germany and the UK.

Some recipes call for rue, which I have left out because it can be difficult to get, as can savoury, which can also be omitted. You can add 2 teaspoons of finely chopped fennel instead. Use hog or sheep skins (22 and 18 mm diameter respectively).

1 kg belly pork
150 g pork back fat
150 g almonds
20 g chopped parsley
2 teaspoons chopped savoury
2 teaspoons curing salt
2 teaspoons crushed black pepper
2 teaspoons cumin
150 ml chilled red wine
20 ml Thai fish sauce

1. Cover and chill the meat and fat for a couple of hours. Cube and grind with the coarse plate, or roughly chop. Transfer to a large bowl.

2. Toast the almonds under the grill on a low heat for 5 minutes, turning (keep an eye on them to make sure they do not burn). Allow to cool before transferring to a food bag. Seal and bash with a rolling pin to a rough consistency. Alternatively, you can crush the almonds in a food processor. Dice the fat to about 3 mm pieces. Use a pestle and mortar to pound all the herbs and spices together. Add to the bowl, together with the red wine and fish sauce. Thoroughly mix before stuffing into casings.

The casings
There is some debate about which casings to use. I have seen some Lucanian sausages made using sheep casings, but personally I prefer hog skins, linked at about 5 cm. If using sheep skins, link at about 10 cm (see also page 35).

The sausages are traditionally smoked and cooked. I prefer to hot smoke them with apple wood chipping and you can easily achieve the same effect on a barbecue, which is a convenient method. You can serve them hot or cold. Alternatively, bake in a preheated oven (180°C/Gas 4) for 25 minutes.

Bolognese sausage
Makes about 8 sausages

A very simple beef sausage with a wonderful flavour. You can add a teaspoon of basil to the sausage mixture, if liked. And you've guessed, it goes well with spaghetti and a Bolognese sauce. Sheep skins (18 mm diameter) will shrink round the stuffing without sagging.

1 kg beef
50 g breadcrumbs
2 teaspoons curing salt
200 g tomato purée
4–6 garlic cloves, grated and crushed
50 ml iced water

1. Cover and chill the beef for a couple of hours, then cube and finely mince. Use the medium plate and then mince again with the fine plate, or mince to a paste in the food processor.

2. Transfer to a large bowl and combine the remaining ingredients, adding the water slowly until the paste is firm but pliant. Squidging through the fingers easily is a good test for the best stuffing consistency.

3. The sausages can be cooked directly in a cassoulet, or in a ragù sauce and served directly. They will freeze in food bags or vacuum packed, and will last for up to 3 months.

Salami
Makes 2 salami

Similar to an Italian-style salami, this sausage is simmered in water to cook. The casings are traditionally ox runners (we used 40 mm diameter).

1 kg shin or skirt of beef, cut into small chunks
1 kg belly pork, skin removed and cut into chunks
25 g curing salt
2 teaspoons caster sugar
2 teaspoons mustard seeds
15 g black pepper, coarsely ground in a pestle and mortar
1 teaspoon cardamom seeds
1 level teaspoon ground ginger
¼ teaspoon grated nutmeg

1. Cover and chill the meat for a couple of hours. Cube and mince the meats together and place in a large mixing bowl.

2. Add the remaining ingredients and mix well with your hands for 2–3 minutes to thoroughly combine.

3. Prepare the individual casings and stuff them well with the mixture (hand stuffing with a small spoon is probably best). Cover and leave for 3–4 hours in the fridge. Tie the bottom of the skin and reinforce it with butcher's twine before you start.

4. Place the sausages in a saucepan of simmering water and cook for 1 hour. Test the temperature inside the sausage: it should read at least 75°C (167°F).

5. Leave to dry at room temperature for a couple of hours and then refrigerate, covered. The salamis will keep in the fridge for up to a week.

Air-dried salami
Makes 2 salami

This sausage is similar to the chorizo on page 111 in as much as you use a microbial starter as a part of the process. Please see the notes on chorizo regarding this (page 107). Use 40 mm diameter ox runners for skins.

1 kg lean beef
1 kg pork shoulder
300 g pork fat
30 g curing salt
25 g white pepper
25 g sugar
4–6 garlic cloves, grated and crushed
½ teaspoon acidophilus starter or other available sausage starter
200 ml chilled red wine

1. Cover and chill the meat and fat in the freezer for an hour or so until it is almost but not quite frozen. Your grinder should be kept cold too. Grind the meat very finely but keep the fat in small chunks, 4 mm across. Transfer to a bowl, then combine the remaining ingredients, ensuring the contents are well mixed and cool (I set the bowl on ice in a washing up bowl).

2. Use a small spoon to stuff into casings. Tie off each link, which should be around 30 cm long (see also page 37). Leave at room temperature for 24 hours before hanging in a cool area for 8 weeks, at 75 per cent relative humidity and around 12°C (54°F). The salami will be ready when it is dry, it can be cut through with some resistance and when there is a uniform consistency.

3. The basic idea of the above salami is now changeable to make all sorts of sausage. It is important that you keep the salt content to between 2.5 and 3.5 per cent – you can safely go down to the lower end of this if you use curing salt.

4. There are a number of checks you can do to make sure the sausage is working well below and see also the advice on chorizo (page 112):

Acidity

On the whole, the sausage should start at about pH 7. As the starter microbes work in the acidity should increase (and therefore the pH number should decrease) so by the month's end it should be around pH5.

Weight

The sausage should lose weight through the evaporation of water. Weight loss should be around 30 per cent so weigh the sausage after the 24-hour incubation period and then again when you think it is ready.

Look out for mould

Depending on the starter culture you use, the sausage should bloom and will usually have a white-ish coating. Any furring can be wiped away with a piece of kitchen roll soaked in vinegar. Discard any sausages that are black or smelly, oozing and/or unusually soft, or have any other striking unusual colour on the surface.

Pets and children

Make sure the sausage is stored safely away from pets and other creatures such as rats and mice. Also, children should understand the sausage is potentially dangerous until it is finished and shown to be safe.

A really important point is flies – they don't care a jot about salt, so be sure to keep the developing sausages free from flying insects.

Turkish and Greek

Influences from mainland Europe, Africa and the Middle East have given Turkey and Greece an amazing variety of cured meat products, some of which have found their way into modern European sausage cuisine. Still more resemble what we would call 'kebab' but are essentially sausages. Most of the recipes go back to the invasions of Genghis Khan.

Pork and feta
Makes 6–8 sausages

This recipe went down a storm at a party we once had – the sausages were so completely edible I didn't get a look in! The ones I made then had garlic in them too (about four crushed cloves), but here I have left it out. For a fine bite use 18 mm diameter sheep casings.

1 kg pork shoulder
150 g feta cheese
3 tablespoons tomato purée
100 g breadcrumbs
100 ml water
30 ml olive oil or sun-dried tomato oil
2 teaspoons curing salt
50 g finely chopped sun-dried tomatoes

1. Cover and chill the pork for a couple of hours before dicing and grinding with the coarse plate.

2. Chop the feta into as small pieces as possible. Transfer to a large bowl with the pork. Add the remaining ingredients and mix together thoroughly to combine. Cover and leave in the fridge overnight to infuse.

3. Stuff into sheep casings, stuffed from the grinder and linked by twisting at about 15 cm (see also page 35). Bake in a preheated oven (180°C/Gas 4) for about 25 minutes. The sausages will freeze in freezer bags or vacuum packs for up to 3 months.

Lucaniko
Makes about 12 sausages

Basically of Greek origin, this air-dried sausage containing the herb savoury is found in the outlying Macedonian areas, and as far inland as Bulgaria. Similar to Bulgarian sujuk, it can be sliced like salami. Use 28mm diameter hog casings.

1.5 kg minced pork
500 g minced beef or lamb
25 g curing salt
2 rounded tablespoons ground cumin
½–1 teaspoon ground black pepper
1 level tablespoon sweet paprika
2 tablespoons savoury, finely chopped
100 ml iced water

1. Cover and chill the meats for a couple of hours before dicing and grinding them together using the medium plate, or fairly roughly in the food processor.

2. Transfer to a large mixing bowl and add the remaining ingredients. Massage well into the meat with your hands, making sure everything is well combined. Cover the bowl and leave in the fridge for 24 hours.

3. Prepare the casings for stuffing as you require and slowly fill, packing the skins well with sausage meat until they are as full as possible without splitting them. Link into long sausage shapes about 30 cm long and flatten to form an oval rather than a cylindrical shape. Use a rolling pin to help flatten the sausage, rolling it lengthways up and down gently.

4. Hang the sausages in a cool dry place and leave for about two weeks. Prick out any air with a sterile sewing needle, if necessary. After this period the sausages are then cooked before eating. Bake in a preheated oven (180°C/Gas 4) for about 25 minutes, or the sausages can be cooked in a casserole directly.

Sucuck
Makes 4 sausages

A typically fermented sausage from Turkey, made from beef and lamb. It is sometimes smoked, other times eaten plain, cooked in stews, sliced onto pitta and salad or simply eaten cold.

This version is not fermented, and therefore cannot really be called anything but an approximation. The reason for not fermenting the sausage is that it does not store well in temperate conditions, and most sausage makers will not have the correct humidity controlled cabinets. It is harder to keep than chorizo. Also, this sausage needs a starter that increases the acidity of the sausage, as used with fermented chorizo, but here we are using vinegar to give that tang.

The cured sausage is highly salted, and since we are going to cook this sausage, there is no need for so much salt. Our version uses far less salt, although the salt is still quite high compared to other sausages in this book. Use beef runner casings at 40 mm diameter.

1 kg shin beef
1 kg lamb shoulder
2 teaspoons black pepper
2 teaspoons cayenne pepper
12 garlic cloves
15 g ground cumin
20 ml olive oil

1. Cover and cool the meat for a couple of hours. Chop and grind using the coarse plate of your grinder, or fairly loosely with a food processor. Transfer to a large mixing bowl.

2. Add the remaining ingredients and mix well with your hands (you may wish to wear gloves at this stage). Take your time to ensure a thorough mix.

3. Soak the beef runner skins in the usual way and then knot one end and stuff the sausage meat in the usual way. Link the sausages at around 30 cm, reinforcing the links with butcher's twine. Tie the other end of the sausage (see also page 51). Place on a baking tray and bake in a preheated oven at 180°C (Gas 4) for about 40 minutes. After 20 minutes' cooking time reduce the heat to 160°C (Gas 3). It is important to check the internal temperature of these sausages: they should reach 75°C (167°F) for 10 minutes before allowing to cool.

4. Alternatively, store by freezing in freezer bags or better still, vacuum pack. They will last three months in the freezer, or a week in the fridge.

Sheftalia
Makes about 10 sausages

Another archetypal Greek sausage not dissimilar to a burger except these sausages are traditionally wrapped in caul fat, a membrane that holds the internal organs in place and made from protein and fat. In effect it's non-bubbly bubble wrap in your body! You can get it from all good butchers (usually in sheets) but you will probably have to order it. The sausage is prepared and cooked straight away for immediate consumption. However, it can be kept, covered, in the fridge for up to five days.

1 kg pork shoulder
1 large onion
50 g freshly chopped parsley
Salt and pepper to taste
20 ml vinegar
1 x 40 cm sheet caul

1. Cover and chill the meat in the fridge for a couple of hours. The meat is roughly ground (use the medium plate) and then combined with the remaining ingredients in a large bowl.

2. Roll tablespoon pieces of the mixture in caul fat to make sausages. These are then baked in a preheated oven at 160°C (Gas 3) for 20 minutes.

Chapter 7
Eastern European sausages

Still today in many Polish or Romanian villages the killing of a pig is a community affair, witnessed by young and old alike, and the making of sausages is a treat for all concerned. Eastern European sausage makers are masters of economy, using ingredients such as potato and cabbage in their sausages to bulk them out.

Polish kielbasa
Makes about 3 sausages

This sausage is simmered and can be eaten straight away or kept in the fridge and fried or grilled later. Use small hog skins at 22 mm diameter.

2 kg pork shoulder, coarsely ground with some of
the fat (about 15 per cent)
1 teaspoon mustard seeds
½ teaspoon grated nutmeg
1 tablespoon salt
1 teaspoon ground white pepper
1 teaspoon marjoram
2–3 garlic cloves, chopped
150 ml water

1. Cover and chill the meat for a couple of hours before cubing and grinding it coarsely, using the medium plate in the grinder. Place the meat in a large mixing bowl.

2. Put the mustard seeds, nutmeg, seasoning and marjoram in a small dish and mix together well.

3. Spread the meat out on a work surface and push holes in it with your fingertips. Sprinkle the spice and herb mix all over the meat and then add the garlic. Massage in well to distribute the seasoning. Add the water and mix well.

4. Prepare your casings and your chosen method of stuffing and stuff the casings. Twist into 40 cm lengths and form into rings. Join the ends together with butcher's twine (see also page 51). Simmer the sausages in a large pan for 25–30 minutes then fry in oil or butter to serve.

5. The sausages can be placed in freezer bags or vacuum packs and will freeze for up to three months.

Kabano-style sausage
Makes 12–15 sausages

An air-dried and smoked sausage, this is usually long and thin so uses 18 mm diameter sheep casings.

2 kg pork shoulder
500 g uncooked ham or gammon
1 tablespoon salt
1 teaspoon black pepper
2 garlic cloves, chopped
¼ teaspoon grated nutmeg
1 level teaspoon caraway seeds

1. Cover and chill the meats for a couple of hours before mincing together as finely as you can. Grind first using the medium plate and then again with the fine plate, or work to a paste with a food processor.

2. Transfer to a mixing bowl and press holes in it with your fingertips. Sprinkle the remaining ingredients evenly over the top and mix well with your hands. Massage the meat for about 4 minutes to make it paste-like.

3. Prepare the casings and your chosen method of stuffing. Stuff the casings well and evenly before linking into long sausages, about 30cm long (see also page 35).

4. Hang the sausages in a very dry, cool place for about 12 hours to dry the outer casings. Though traditionally smoked, I prefer to cook the sausages in a preheated oven (180°C/Gas 4) for 15 minutes, allowing them to cool before serving.

Cevaps
Makes 12–15 sausages

This is a Croatian sausage, popular in much of Eastern Europe. A mixed meat sausage that does not require a casing, it is rolled together and cut into sausage lengths. It is best not to roll too much mixture at any one time to give greater control of the shape. The garlic and salt content is variable and to taste, the amounts here are given as a guide. Spice up with the addition of half a teaspoon of chilli pepper, or a tablespoon of paprika, if liked.

This sausage marks the halfway house between what we would recognise as sausages and kebabs, particularly shish. Though often cooked on an open charcoal grill or barbecue, they can be conventionally grilled or fried in a shallow pan. Yoghurt or raita is the usual accompaniment.

500 g minced beef
250 g minced pork
250 g minced lamb
1–3 garlic cloves, chopped
1 medium onion, finely chopped
7 g curing salt

1. First, cover and chill the meat for a couple of hours. It then needs to be cubed and coarsely ground. Grind with the medium plate in your grinder or roughly in a food processor.

2. Place the meat, garlic, onion and salt in a large mixing bowl and massage everything together, making sure it is thoroughly mixed. Cover and leave in a refrigerator for 1 hour.

3. Using half the mixture, roll out a 2 cm diameter sausage and repeat with the other half. Cut sections of the meat to make even-sized sausages, around 7 cm long. Arrange on a plate or in a shallow dish and cover. Place in the fridge for another hour or until ready to cook. Remove from the fridge about 30 minutes before cooking to bring to room temperature. The sausages may also be frozen for up to three months at this stage in freezer bags or vacuum packs.

4. Grill under a medium heat, turning frequently. Check the internal temperature with a probe thermometer (it should read 75°C/167°F) or slice and inspect for thorough cooking. Although best grilled, the sausages can also be fried (for about 15 minutes) in a pan with a very little oil over a low heat.

Droby
Makes 15–18 sausages

Potato and pork sausage is a common European sausage which can have almost anything in it – sometimes bacon, pieces of ham, even beef. It evolved to make whatever was at hand in the kitchen go a long way. Here, potato is used as a filler, which makes this a real peasant meal.

There are essentially two ways of doing this. The vegetable portion (such as potatoes) can be blitzed in the food processor or grinder and the raw potato then added to the pork and other ingredients. The other way is to bake the potatoes in their skins until soft and then scoop out the pulp. This does impart a slightly different flavour to the sausage.

You can amend this method of creating sausages, which although not actually made from leftovers are designed to make a little go a long way. This sausage does keep in the freezer (in freezer bags or vacuum packs for up to three months), but do not leave it long at room temperature or in the fridge, covered, for up to a week. In this case it is best to use ordinary salt as opposed to the curing variety. Use 28 mm diameter hog casings.

500 g pork shoulder, chopped
A little oil for frying
300 g unsmoked bacon, diced (or try smoked bacon for
a different flavour)
2 medium onions, finely chopped
2 kg potatoes, diced
15 g salt
1 teaspoon ground black pepper
1 teaspoon dried marjoram
½ teaspoon dried or 1 teaspoon chopped fresh mint

1. First, cook the pork in simmering water until tender for about 30 minutes. Lift the meat out of the water and set to one side. Reserve the cooking water.

2. Heat some oil in a large frying pan and gently fry the bacon. After 3–4 minutes add the onions and fry until softened without browning.

3. Put the pork and diced potatoes in a food processor or meat grinder and mince together.

4. Transfer the bacon and onion mixture to a large mixing bowl and sprinkle over the remaining ingredients. Add the pork and potato mixture and mix well with your hands to ensure the seasonings are well distributed. Add a little of the meat liquor left over from cooking the pork to make a pliant mixture – this will help when filling the casings.

5. Prepare the casings and your chosen stuffing method and fill the casings with the meat and potato mixture. Link at about 15 cm (see also page 35). Cover and leave in a cool dry place for 3 hours.

6. The sausages can then be shallow fried in a little oil for about 10 minutes, gently turning or simmer in a pan of hot water for about 40 minutes. Alternatively, arrange on a greased roasting tin and bake for about 45 minutes at 180°C (Gas 4). Do make sure they are thoroughly cooked – potato can be both a good insulator, and food for spoiling bacteria. Test them with a meat thermometer (it should read 75°C/167°F) or slice and ensure they are piping hot.

7. You can also freeze the sausages in bags or vacuum pack for up to three months before cooking.

Polony with mace
Makes about 4 sausages

This recipe was given to me by my friend Derek Senior. Polony is essentially an Eastern European sausage, often with a lot of fat incorporated in it. This ingredient came from the time when pigs were fed in such a way as to fatten them up. Pigs these days are much leaner, and therefore there is not so much interest in fat.
Use 28 mm diameter hog skins for the casings.

1 kg pork leg or shoulder about 80/20 lean/fat
17 g curing salt
2.5 g mace
6 g white pepper
1 g nutmeg
1 g coriander
½ teaspoon cinnamon
100 g rusk (I used pinhead and ground them down)
200 g water

1. Cover and chill the meat for about an hour in the fridge. Remove the skin and gristle from the meat; also any stringy bits and mince through the fine plate on the mincer.

2. Put all the seasonings and rusk in a bag and shake well to combine. Transfer to a bowl, add the water and mix together. Leave to rest for a few minutes: you will find the mixture has stuck together. With the palms of your hands crumble it up into a breadcrumb consistency. Add the meat and mix thoroughly.

3. Grind the mixture down in a food processor (do this in batches): you are looking for a smooth paste consistency. Once completed give the mixture a good stir. If it seems a little firm, add more water to loosen.

4. I use hog skins for the casing and cut them into 45 cm lengths (about 6 should suffice). You will need 12 pieces of butcher's twine to tie the ends. Put the skins and the string in to soak (this prevents the string from stretching and coming loose when boiled).

5. Put the filling into a sausage stuffer. Tie one end of the skins and feed it onto the nozzle, then fill to a firm sausage, being careful not to overfill so they burst when handling. By keeping the meat up to the end of the tube it should pass any air that is trapped out along the skin. Once the skin is filled tie off nice and tightly with the string and then fasten the two ends together to form a ring.

6. Fill a pan large enough to take the whole batch of sausages with water. Heat to 27°C (80°F). Heat the water, add the sausage and heat, uncovered, until the water is 27°C (80°F) again then cook for 40 minutes. They will be full, plump and slightly hard. Don't let the water boil over as it could cause the skins to split. When cooked, drain off the hot water and fill the pan with cold water to quickly cool down the sausages.

7. The sausages are eaten cold. Once cooled, they can be placed in freezer bags or vacuum wrapped, then frozen. They will last in the freezer for up to three months.

Hungarian hazi kolvasz
Makes about 12 sausages

This tasty, paprika-based sausage is oven-baked. It stays moist because it is cooked with a little water surrounding it in a roasting tin. You could also use a good ale or beer instead to add a certain bitterness and hop flavour. Use 28 mm diameter hog casings.

2 kg pork shoulder, coarsely ground
3 garlic cloves, grated or crushed
25 g curing salt
1 teaspoon ground black pepper
1 tablespoon sweet paprika
125 ml water
A little oil for frying and greasing

1. Cover and chill the meat for a couple of hours, then cube and roughly grind with the medium plate, or roughly in the food processor.

2. In a small bowl mix together the garlic, salt, pepper, paprika and water. Whisk together and set aside.

3. Transfer the meat to a large mixing bowl and make holes all over the surface with your fingertips to allow the liquid and spices to reach all parts. Pour the liquid spice mix over the meat and use your hands to massage well into the meat. Test a small patty of the meat by frying it and adjust the seasoning as necessary.

4. Leave the meat covered in the fridge while you prepare the casings and stuffing method. Run your hands under a cold tap and keeping them moist fill the casings with the prepared meat mixture. Link the sausages to the required size, about 15 cm long (see also page 35). Leave to rest in the fridge for 1 hour, then remove and leave covered at room temperature for 30 minutes before cooking.

5. Preheat the oven to 160°C (Gas 3). Place the sausage in a greased roasting tin with a little space between each one and pour in a little water to keep moist. Bake for about 45 minutes until the sausages are evenly browned. Avoid overcooking as they will dry out. Once cooked, the sausages can be eaten immediately, sliced cold or added to other dishes. They may also be frozen prior to cooking. Freeze in freezer bags or vacuum wrap before freezing and they will last up to three months.

Mititei
Makes 20–24 sausages

Coming from Romania, Mititei means 'wee ones' and that is just what they are: small skinless sausages that are good for frying or barbecuing. They can just as easily be fashioned into burger shapes, although these are in fact always referred to as sausages in Romania.

750 g pork shoulder
750 g lamb
3 garlic cloves, chopped
4 ice cubes
½ teaspoon thyme
½ teaspoon chilli powder
1 rounded teaspoon good-quality smoked paprika
2 teaspoons caraway seeds
15 g curing salt

1. Cover and chill the meat for a couple of hours, then cube and roughly mince it together in a bowl. Combine well. Add the garlic and mix in.

2. Wrap the ice cubes in a tea towel and crush with a rolling pin. Alternatively, crush in the food processor. Mix the remaining ingredients together in a dish and sprinkle over the meat and crushed ice cubes. Massage the mixture in well with your hands to evenly distribute all the herbs and spices. Cover the bowl, place in the fridge and leave for 6 hours.

3. Using moist hands, divide the meat mixture into 20–24 little balls then form into sausage shapes, about 7 cm long. Grill, oven-bake at 180°C (Gas 4) for 25 minutes, or alternatively, you can fry or barbecue gently. They can be eaten hot or cold.

4. The sausages can be placed in freezer bags or vacuum packs and frozen for up to three months.

Chapter 8

Dishes using sausages, sauces and accompaniments

This chapter is about some of the uses of sausages and how the manufacture of the sausage matches that use. You will soon discover there are lots of reasons why some sausages are very large while others are narrow, long and hard. There is more to sausages than their geographical origins.

I suppose what follows is the answer to the common question, 'Can I make a 100 per cent meat sausage?' Well, you might just as well eat the meat itself! All the ingredients of sausages, wherever they are made, are there for a reason, and this includes materials one might mistakenly consider to be fillers. As we repeatedly encounter in this book, there is no need for fillers in sausages. Even the simplest breakfast sausage is one of the more intricate food products we eat, comparable to cheese and more complex pies. Consequently, every sausage is an evolution of trial and error over many generations to give you the various types. Thick-skinned sausages are made in this way because of how they are eaten, how they are stored and so on as opposed to thin-skinned sausages, which have a completely different culinary niche.

Bangers

It is amazing that the Second World War still affects the way we look at sausages in the UK. They are an example of how the envelope of manufacture was stretched too far. Sausages were made with very little in the way of meat, and larger amounts of breadcrumbs and water. No one bothered to experiment with them because they were made mostly by independent corner shop butchers. The result was the extra water built up steam in the cooking sausage, which caused them to explode (bang!), hence the name.

The remedy was to stab the sausages prior to cooking, causing the release of excess water – and also flavour for that matter. However, some seventy years later the water content of sausages is much more reasonable, and they no longer explode. Pricking sausages only allows the flavoursome juices to escape and consequently makes the cooking process more difficult. So, please don't prick your sausages! Cook them slowly, for a long time, and they will be perfect.

Types of sausage for cooking
Sausages for casseroles

Cassoulet from the South West of France is the archetypal casserole using sausage. The Romans too had a favourite stew of mutton and beans flavoured with fish sauce, wine and tomatoes. Over the years a number of other ingredients have been introduced to make the dish what it is today, and to be honest, it depends on which village you visit as to what the recipe actually is.

The majority of recipes include pork of some kind. Many include duck confit, all include haricot beans (though the Romans didn't have haricot beans, they came much later) and sausage.

Like all sausages made for boiling, the Toulouse sausage is made with hog skins. The last thing you want is the skin breaking and the contents spilling out, so a strong skin is required. The link of a Toulouse sausage is very firmly tied with a knot, and sometimes with butcher's string, so the contents are firmly held in place and the skins are not particularly heavily filled.

The recipe for the Toulouse sausage calls for an equal amount of sugar to salt, and the saltiness is a little higher than normal. It contains garlic, nutmeg and wine but no breadcrumbs or rusk. In a way the sausage is used to season the casserole and the final levels of saltiness and other seasonings are made up towards the end of the cooking process. The sausages are added uncut, that is as a string, and when the dish is served, the cuts of meat are cut up as part of the stew.

Toulouse sausage cassoulet
Serves 4

Use either canned haricot beans or dried ones soaked overnight in cold water. The secret of this dish is to cook it long and slow. Serve this with baked potatoes, or with hearty chunks of bread.

2 tablespoons olive oil
4 rashers streaky bacon, chopped
450 g Toulouse sausages (page 84)
1 medium onion, chopped
2 garlic cloves, chopped
1 stick celery, chopped
1 large carrot, chopped
400 g can haricot beans or 280 g dried beans, soaked
overnight in cold water
400 g can chopped tomatoes
500 ml water or chicken stock
1 teaspoon dried parsley
Salt and pepper to taste
50 g lightly toasted breadcrumbs
1 tablespoon chopped fresh parsley

1. Preheat the oven to 150°C (Gas 2).

2. Heat the oil in a large frying pan and fry the bacon and sausages until lightly browned. Place in a large lidded casserole dish. Retain the oils in the pan.

3. In the same pan, fry the onion and garlic for a few minutes over a medium heat then add the celery and carrot. Stir in the beans and tomatoes then pour the mixture over the sausages. Add the water or stock and season to taste, stirring. Cover with the lid and cook for 2–2½ hours.

4. Remove the lid and sprinkle over the breadcrumbs and parsley. Return to the oven and cook uncovered for 1 hour or until the sauce in the casserole has thickened and the beans are very soft.

The pizza

The popularity of the pizza is worldwide, and many sausage versions of this product are available – mostly highly flavoured, highly spiced sausages that add not only heat but also seasoning to the dish. Tomatoes, one of the fundamentals of the pizza, are particularly salt-hungry, and with cheese and other toppings the pizza makes a big dent in your daily salt allowance.

On the whole, the sausages used on pizza are Eastern European in origin, the salamis and polony types, or are Mediterranean in origin, such as the chorizo. But mostly these sausages have been modified to give an American feel.

Over the years the hot and spicy pizza has developed to almost a fine art. Essentially the combination of freshly baked dough, tomatoes, cheese and basil that makes the classic Margherita has had to compete with stronger flavours to remain interesting. The sausages used are therefore highly spiced, with a lot of chilli and paprika, used in comparatively small amounts to give the pizza extra flavour. What was once a pizza with salami has given way to pizza with much stronger sausage, nduja.

The nduja is almost a pâté in a skin rather than a sausage. Versions exist where the sausage is cut open and the contents scooped out. They are made in either hog or collagen skins and have little bite. The last thing you want is a sausage skin causing you to have problems with the pizza topping! There is a frighteningly high amount of ground chilli in the sausage, making it more or less a condiment although I am sure there are people out there who can eat them whole.

The traditional sausage pizza is a more modest affair, if there is such a thing as a traditional pizza. For this recipe the sausage of choice is the kabano, mostly because it is stuffed into sheep skins and is therefore small with hardly any bite associated with the skin. They are usually smoked, cooked and dried, and are easy to make at home.

There is a lot of pepper in the kabano sausage and around 2 per cent salt. Some recipes only call for this combination, but others include nutmeg and caraway. They are folded into links that are 60 cm long and tied at the ends to dry.

Kabano pizza
This quantity of dough makes 2 large or 3 medium pizzas

For the dough
1 kg strong flour
2 teaspoons salt
1 x 7g sachet fast action dried yeast
About 600 ml warm water
1 tablespoon sunflower, rapeseed or olive oil, plus extra for greasing
A little flour for working the dough

For the tomato sauce
300 ml passata
1 tablespoon tomato purée
1 garlic clove, grated
1 teaspoon dried oregano
1 or 2 kabano sausages

1. Sieve together the flour and salt into a large mixing bowl. Stir in the yeast and make a well in the centre of the flour. Pour in half of the water and the oil and stir into the flour with a long-handled spoon, adding more water until the dough becomes soft but not too sticky. After the first mixing with the spoon use your hands to bring the dough together.

2. Start to knead the dough in the bowl until it forms a smooth ball. Transfer to a lightly floured work surface and knead for 5 minutes. Place in a covered bowl at room temperature and set to one side for 15 minutes. Cut the dough into two equal portions and roll out, as thickly as you like, to fit two large oiled trays. I usually use two large baking trays or three 23 cm round pizza trays.

3. Preheat the oven to 220°C (Gas 7) for at least 10 minutes (pizzas are best cooked in an extremely hot oven). Mix all the ingredients for the tomato topping in a jug with a fork or small balloon whisk. With a palette knife, smooth about 5–6 tablespoons of topping over the pizza bases right to the edges

and top with your favourite cheese and other ingredients. Always be generous with your topping, but leave a border of about 2 cm of plain dough around the edges or the topping will melt over.

Toppings

For the toppings don't restrict yourself to just mozzarella cheese, try Cheddar, Red Leicester, Monterey Jack ... even a crumbly Lancashire is delicious. A mixture is what we prefer. Don't even bother grating it if you don't wish to, small chunks or slices are fine. Chop your sausage into 3–5 mm pieces and liberally sprinkle over the pizza. Add a little torn basil and black pepper, if liked.

Bake for around 15 minutes, checking as you go. The cheese should be melted and hot, but not so the oil escapes from the curd or the sausage. When sliced, the cheese should string in the old-fashioned mozzarella way. Crumbly cheese, such as homemade ricotta, added to the mix gives little creamy bombshells of flavour.

Sausage and pasta dishes

Poor man's heaven, and I mean heaven. Pasta dishes, either ragù based, with lots of tomatoes, or dairy based carbonara, lend themselves to sausage as an ingredient.

One of the most common errors made is to add too much flavour, especially with cream sauces. The resulting combination can often be sickly. Using chorizo with a carbonara sauce, for example, is fine so long as you do not use too much. A highlight flavour with, say, ham or seafood is perfect; the paprika also imparts a pleasing orange colour. Similarly with meat sauces, lamb mince or a combination of lamb and pork or beef can be highlighted by a few pieces of a spicy sausage.

An excellent sausage-based ingredient for a tomato sauce is good old-fashioned Cumberland, cooked as a ring and with the addition of a tomato sauce with garlic. The main flavour of Cumberland is pepper, black and white, and sometimes (depending on where you are in the North West of England) a little sage. These thick sausages are stuffed into hog skins and are very robust. They have a lower breadcrumb percentage but are still very substantial.

Cumberland savoury penne
Serves 4

1 Cumberland ring or sausages to 500 g (page 62)
A little oil for frying
2 garlic cloves, crushed
100 ml chicken stock (or white wine or a mixture of both)
2 tablespoons tomato purée
400 g chopped tomatoes (can be tinned)
Salt and pepper to taste
500 g penne

1. First, slice the sausage into 2.5 cm pieces. Heat some oil in a pan and fry the sausage and crushed garlic until completely cooked. Start with the sausage, adding the garlic later to avoid it burning and taking on a bitter flavour.

2. Add the stock, tomato purée and tomatoes then simmer for 15 minutes. Season to taste.

3. Meanwhile, prepare the penne according to the directions on the package and combine with the sauce to serve. The dish can be topped with cheese and finished off under the grill. We almost always use homemade Cheshire or farmhouse Cheddar. Brie is completely wonderful and some stilton crumbled at the last minute is totally amazing.

Sausage carbonara
Serves 4

This is a bit of a cheat, but it does illustrate a use for sausage that goes back to its origin. Carbonara meatballs is a classic dish, but this recipe uses scooped-out sausage meat to make a somewhat tastier version. You can use any sausage meat you like, or indeed buy sausage meat specially for the purpose. I like to use our homemade breakfast sausage (page 32), but rather than simply stuffing the meat and then breaking the skins I use a part of a sausage making session to make the meatballs, and freeze them separately.

Actually I have started to put the meat into ice cube trays for this purpose (it will freeze for up to three months) and when I am ready to cook, I simply pop a tray out to defrost. Either way, once I have my sausage meat (about 500 g), I add two crushed cloves of garlic.

A little oil for frying
500 g sausage meat in small balls, around 2.5cm
100 ml single cream
2 medium eggs and 2 yolks
Salt and pepper to taste
400 g pasta (ribbons of any type)
150 g grated cheese (Pecorino is good, but then so too is Cheddar)

1. Heat some oil in a frying pan and then fry the sausage meat, making sure it is completely cooked through.

2. Meanwhile, in a mixing bowl combine the cream and eggs and beat together. Season with salt and pepper.

3. Cook the pasta in boiling salted water according to the package directions.

4. Once the pasta is cooked, drain and add the meatballs and egg and cream mixture. Mix together very well. Serve at once with cheese sprinkled on top.

Sausage ravioli
Serves 2–4

Much of the ravioli you get in the shops is more or less sausage meat in a pasta shell. It is precooked and skinless, often beef, sometimes lamb or pork. A really special version can be made at home, and it is really simply to do. Brilliant with a cheese sauce.

For the pasta
6 medium eggs
500 g strong flour for breadmaking (use '00' flour
if you like), plus extra for rolling out

For the filling
1 chorizo sausage (30 cm long)
About 200 g mozzarella

1. Simply crack the eggs into a bowl and beat together. Sieve the flour into a mixing bowl and make a well in the centre. Add the beaten egg a little at a time and incorporate with your fingertips. Keep on mixing and kneading until you have a smooth lump of pasta.

2. Roll out two thin sheets of pasta, about 30 cm and square-ish. The first is laid on a floured work surface.

3. Slice the chorizo into 3 mm pieces and create equally sized pieces of mozzarella cheese. Place the sausage on the pasta and then the mozzarella on top spaced at intervals (allow a teaspoon of the mixture for each ravioli piece). Brush water around each heap of filing.

4. Cover with the second sheet of pasta and then press together to make the sealed joins of each raviolo. Use a knife to cut out 4 cm squarish shapes. Boil for two to three minutes until the pasta is cooked.

Hot dogs

The Wiener and the Berliner sausages were once staple German street foods and were transported to the USA by immigrants. Essentially the original sausage was served with sauerkraut on a bun, but in time this was supplanted by pickles of various sorts, mostly mustard.

The whole idea of the hot dog was for the consumer to have a quick and convenient meal on the move. In particular, it was produced in a sheep skin for the softness of bite – nothing to distract from the effect of biting through the sausage and bun in one movement. Supermarket Wieners are mostly packed in collagen skins.

Most hot dogs are now mass-produced from a combination of pork bits (honestly, bits) and chicken carcasses (you don't want to know!). Those tinned in brine are boiled in the canning process and taste of metallic substances. Their pinkness is due to the addition of cochineal.

A genuine Wiener sausage is much more pleasant, and these are stuffed into sheep skins. You can get them from many delis or make your own (page 104). They are quite simple, being lightly spiced and often smoked. There are two ways of serving them in the traditional fashion. First is on a bun with coleslaw spooned over the sausage or, alternatively, you can serve with no bun on a bed of sauerkraut with mashed potato on the side.

Offal sausages

When I was a child I used to 'help out' at an abattoir. Such a thing would not be allowed these days, and whereas the owner wouldn't let us near the place when he was actually killing, he would pay us to hose down the yard and muck out the pens.

I have to confess that we used to 'play war' (something children don't tend to do these days, we would recreate the latest Western film we had seen at Saturday morning pictures) and I remember being shouted at for using a pig's testicle (from a bucket of them) as a hand grenade. 'They're going for sausages!'

I never asked about them again even though I often wondered what sausages they were being used for – and I still don't know. Nor did I realise the black pudding was blood, nor the haggis I loved was sheep's lights (lungs) and barley.

Offal sausages have long been a staple relied on by many poor people. From the Middle Ages every cottager kept a pig, largely for sale to the local abbot, leaving the offal for sausage making. Consequently, there are a large number of offal sausages in the European repertoire. These days there is something of a resurgence in popularity of offal sausages and offal in general.

Onion sauce
Serves 4

It is impossible to imagine a fried sausage without onion sauce, either dark, caramelised and savoury, served with fresh vegetables, or white, creamy and sweet with mashed potatoes.

2 tablespoons sunflower, rapeseed or olive oil
2 medium onions, finely chopped
500 ml milk
1 teaspoon English mustard
Salt and pepper to taste
1 rounded tablespoon cornflour mixed with 3 tablespoons milk

1. Heat the oil in a frying pan and fry the onions very gently until they are soft. Don't allow them to brown.

2. While the onions are cooking heat the milk in a pan to appox 75°C (167°F). Stir the mustard into the hot milk and pour over the onions. Season to taste.

3. Stir in the cornflour paste and bring to the boil, stirring all the time. Turn down the heat and simmer for 3 minutes, then remove from the heat and allow to rest for 5 minutes. Stir once more before serving in a hot jug.

British sausages

On the whole, the traditional British sausages are cooked in the same way as other sausages … slowly! Of course everyone knows fried, grilled and baked versions of the cooked, let's say breakfast, sausage.

If frying in a little oil, use a medium light oil to start to caramelise the outside portion and then turn the heat down to cook the interior. When grilling, keep it low and keep the sausages on the move to prevent burning. If baking, keep the temperature at around 160°C (Gas 3).

One important aspect of cooking British sausages, as we have already hinted at, is the business of pricking. My mother regularly stabbed sausages with a fork before cooking. On no account should this be done with modern sausages, even the cheap ones. It simply allows the juices to escape, makes the sausage somewhat less juicy and certainly less flavoursome.

How to know when sausages are cooked

Generally there is a change in the colour of the sausage meat, but this is not a guide to how well a sausage is cooked. By far the best way of testing is to use a thermometer. Any meat thermometer will do and you are looking for a temperature of 75°C (167°F) for ten minutes. Rest the sausage for three minutes before serving.

Of course traditionally there are some must-have recipes for sausages, apart from the classic 'Full English' and its variations. There are two versions of bangers and mash, one with onion gravy, which is dark, rich and salty, poured in great volumes over sausage and mashed potato. The other is a white sauce, treated in just the same way. Here are two onion gravy recipes – I make both and love them equally. The first is a more glamorous version maybe, but both taste great.

Onion gravy I
Serves 4

A rich accompaniment to sausages, you can omit the red wine if you wish but it adds flavour to the gravy like nothing else.

15 g butter
1 tablespoon sunflower oil
2 medium onions, finely chopped
2 garlic cloves, chopped
2 tablespoons water
2 tablespoons balsamic vinegar
2 level tablespoons plain flour
300 ml warm vegetable or chicken stock
50 ml red wine

1. Heat a large frying pan with the butter and oil. When the butter has melted add the onions and garlic and fry gently until soft, without browning.

2. Sprinkle over the water, turn the heat down and cover with foil or a lid. Cook for 5 more minutes. Sprinkle over the balsamic vinegar and stir well.

3. Stir in the flour and gradually add the stock, stirring, until it is all combined. Stir in the wine and simmer for about 15 minutes until thickened. Serve hot.

Onion gravy II
Serves 4

1 tablespoon sunflower, rapeseed or olive oil
2 medium onions, finely chopped
1 teaspoon soft brown sugar
½–1 teaspoon English mustard
560 ml beef stock (homemade or from a good-quality stock cube)

1. Heat the oil in a pan set over a gentle heat and fry the onions. While they are frying sprinkle over the sugar. Continue to fry, stirring occasionally, over a low heat until the onions begin to caramelise and brown. This will take about 25 minutes.

2. Stir in the mustard and the stock. Bring to the boil and then simmer for about 15 minutes or until the liquid has reduced by about half. Serve hot.

Cumberland sauce
Serves 4–6

Traditionally served with cold roasted meats and ham, but
delicious with sausages too.

200 g redcurrant jelly
150 ml ruby port
Juice and zest of 1 orange and 1 lemon
Pinch cayenne pepper
1 dessertspoon Worcestershire sauce

1. Put the jelly in a saucepan set over a low heat and stir in the
port. Bring to the boil. Reduce the heat and simmer until the
sauce is just runny. Leave to cool for about 10 minutes.

2. Stir in the citrus juices, zest, cayenne pepper and
Worcestershire sauce.

Rich tomato sauce
Serves 4

This is the easiest tomato sauce you could ever make. You can add about a tablespoon of finely chopped basil leaves or another favourite herb while it is simmering at the end.

1 x 500 g carton passata
3 teaspoons golden caster sugar
½ level teaspoon salt
1 teaspoon garlic purée, optional
Black pepper to taste

1. Pour the passata into a small saucepan and stir in the remaining ingredients.

2. Heat gently, stirring constantly until just boiling. Turn the heat down and simmer for 10 minutes to slightly thicken the sauce.

Barbecue sauce
Serves 4

A sweet, sticky sauce that is wonderful to pour over freshly
barbecued sausages.

250 g passata
2 tablespoons tomato purée mixed with 2 tablespoons water
3 tablespoons balsamic vinegar
3 tablespoons honey or golden syrup
2 garlic cloves, chopped
1 tablespoon dark soy sauce
2 tablespoons oyster or hoisin sauce

1. Place all the ingredients in a small saucepan. Bring slowly to
the boil, stirring constantly. Simmer for a few minutes until
thickened.

Mustard sauce
Serves 4

If you need a quick and tasty sauce to go with your sausages here is one for mustard lovers.

280 ml double cream
3 rounded tablespoons Dijon wholegrain mustard
Pinch salt and white pepper

1. Heat all the ingredients together in a saucepan set over a gentle heat, stirring, until the sauce starts to bubble. Turn down the heat to just simmering for 2 minutes, then pour into a warm serving jug.

An easy chutney for sausages (and also good with burgers)
Makes enough for 8 servings

This doesn't make a huge batch, probably only sufficient for six people, but it will keep in the fridge for four to five days if you have any left over.

6 large ripe tomatoes, chopped
½ medium onion, finely chopped
1 garlic clove, chopped
4 tablespoons cider or red or white wine vinegar (whichever you have in your cupboard)
3 tablespoons soft brown sugar
¼ teaspoon each of ground cinnamon, allspice and white pepper
1 level teaspoon salt

1. Place all the ingredients in a sturdy saucepan or preserving pan and heat slowly together until all the sugar has dissolved. Bring to the boil, then cook at a low simmer for 15–20 minutes, occasionally stirring. The chutney should be thick and glossy in appearance.

2. Allow to cool completely before serving – the flavour is much better if you leave it for an hour or two.

Mash ideas

The traditional accompaniment to sausages must be mashed potatoes. Here are some ideas to ring the mash changes.

Irish champ
Serves 4

5 medium potatoes, peeled and cut into chunks
200 ml milk
A knob of butter
6 spring onions, trimmed and chopped
50 g butter
Salt and white pepper to taste

1. Place the potatoes in hot, slightly salted water and bring to the boil, then turn down the heat and simmer for 15–20 minutes until tender.

2. Meanwhile, heat the milk, butter and spring onions in a separate pan until simmering. Simmer gently for 2 minutes, then remove from the heat. Drain the potatoes once cooked and add the butter and seasoning. Mash well and add the onions and some of the milk (25–50 ml maximum) – I don't like too much but it is up to you.

3. Serve hot with sausages.

To vary:
- For Mustard Mash: Cook the potatoes as above but add 3 teaspoons Dijon mustard with the butter and seasoning.
- For Horseradish Mash: Add 3–4 teaspoons creamed horseradish to the potatoes with the butter and salt. Go easy on the pepper, though!

Bubble and squeak
Serves 4

This is a great family favourite. We serve it almost burnt on a plate with fried sausages and fried onions over the top.

50 g butter or lard
2 tablespoons oil
1 small onion, finely chopped
800 g mashed potatoes
300 g cooked green cabbage or Brussels sprouts
Salt and pepper to taste

1. Melt the butter or lard with the oil in a large frying pan. Fry the onion until softened without browning.

2. In a mixing bowl combine the potatoes and green vegetables. Add to the onion and fry for 10–15 minutes, turning the mixture over with a spatula as it browns. Serve immediately.

How to make haggis mash

For a tasty, hearty accompaniment to many winter suppers, or as the delicious topping for shepherd's pie, this haggis mash is a winner. Simply scoop out the contents of a cooked haggis (still hot), and combine with an equal quantity of mashed potato, and a knob of butter.

Basic white sauce

I use three methods of making a white sauce, mainly depending on time as my reason for choosing which one I make. White sauces are usually thickened with flour, either plain or cornflour.

The most traditional method is prepared with a 'roux'. This is a combination of fat – I always use butter – and flour most commonly equal proportions. It gives a rich base to add other ingredients and can be used for savoury or sweet sauces.

A quicker version of this is to put the cold milk, fat and flour into the pan together and whisk like anything. I tend to use more butter than flour in this version as it prevents lumps from forming more readily. The milk has to be cold for this, though or it will go lumpy. This is also a rich base and can be made into savoury or sweet sauces. For both of the above sauces always use plain flour.

The 'cornflour' method uses no fat in its preparation and can lighten the calorie content somewhat. This sauce can be as rich or as light as you wish. You can have a fairly low calorie sauce if you use skimmed milk and no added fat, or add butter to enrich the sauce if that is required. I find this a very versatile way of making a white sauce.

There are no seasonings listed in these recipes as that will depend on what you want to do with the sauce. To flavour these three methods of making a white sauce, the milk may be infused with whatever ingredients you wish (for example, mustard or bay leaves) before preparing the sauce.

White sauce using the roux method
Makes 600ml

40 g butter
40 g plain flour
600 ml warm milk

1. Using a heavy-based pan melt the butter over a low heat and stir in the flour with a wooden spoon or silicone spatula (metal spoons aren't so good for working on lumps). Stir for about 2 minutes without allowing the mixture to colour, so keep over a low heat. This mixture is known as the 'roux'.

2. Remove from the heat. Add the milk slowly and gradually, stirring constantly. When all the milk has been incorporated and the sauce looks smooth, set on a medium heat and stir as the sauce comes to the boil. Turn the heat down to low and cook gently for about 5 minutes, stirring, until the flour is cooked. If this is not done the sauce will taste raw and floury.

3. If there are any lumps in the sauce, simply pass it through a sieve at the end of the cooking time into a warmed jug.

Quick white sauce
Makes 600ml

40 g plain flour
600 ml cold milk
50 g butter

1. Place all the ingredients in a heavy based pan. For best results, sift the flour into the milk. Over a medium heat, stir the sauce with a balloon whisk.

2. Continue to whisk as the sauce comes to the boil, then reduce the heat and cook for 5 minutes, still whisking gently, though. Transfer to a warmed jug.

White sauce using the cornflour method
Makes 600ml

Cornflour cooks more quickly than wheat flour. For a creamy, rich flavour, especially good for sweet sauces, try using a large can of evaporated milk made up to 600ml with water.

600 ml milk (skimmed, semi-skimmed or whole milk)
2 rounded tablespoons cornflour

1. Put about 5 tablespoons of the milk in a clean small jam jar and add the cornflour. Replace the lid tightly and shake until thoroughly combined. This is the easiest way of mixing flour and liquid.

2. Pour the milk into a saucepan pan and heat to approx 75°C (167°F). Add the cornflour mixture and stir well, using a balloon whisk or a wooden spoon. Bring to the boil, stirring constantly, then reduce the heat and simmer for 3–4 minutes.

Toad-in-the-hole
Serves 4

Lard for greasing
180 g plain flour
Good pinch salt
2 medium eggs
600 ml milk
8 thick pork sausages

1. Preheat the oven to 220°C (Gas 7). Grease a large roasting dish with lard.

2. To make the batter, sift the flour and salt together into a mixing bowl and blend in the eggs with a wooden spoon. Gradually whisk in the milk, taking up the flour and egg mixture, and continue whisking for a few minutes. Leave to stand while you prepare the sausages.

3. Lightly brown the sausages in a frying pan then transfer to the greased dish. Put the dish in the oven for 3–4 minutes, then remove from the oven and pour over the batter.

4. Bake immediately for 25–30 minutes then reduce the heat to 200°C (Gas 6) if the batter seems to be cooking too quickly round the edges. The dish is cooked when the batter has risen and is deep golden in colour.

Sausage rolls
Makes 24

One of the best uses for sausage meat – you simply can't beat a sausage roll! It is essentially sausage meat wrapped in rough puff pastry.

Rough puff pastry
450 g plain flour plus extra for rolling out
1 teaspoon salt
340 g chilled butter from the fridge plus extra to grease
150–200 ml cold water
1 egg, beaten, for glazing

1. Sift the flour and salt into a mixing bowl. Add the butter in a whole block and cut into the flour until the pieces are about 1 cm. Alternatively, you can freeze the butter then grate it and stir into the flour.

2. Stir in the water and bring the ingredients together with the knife. Use your hands at the last minute to shape the mixture to form a soft dough.

3. On a floured surface, roll out into a rectangle, 8 x 18 cm. Fold the top third to the centre and the bottom third to the top to meet in the middle. Repeat the process three times and then leave to rest at room temperature for 30 minutes before using.

The filling

Almost any sausage in this book can be used to make a sausage roll. The traditional simple breakfast sausage (page 32) is the best one for ordinary sausage making, but try some Chinese spices, or even a paprika sausage roll.

1 kg diced pork shoulder
150 g breadcrumbs
150 ml water
12 g curing salt
2 g ground black pepper
1 teaspoon mustard powder

1. Preheat the oven to 200°C (Gas 6). Meanwhile, on a floured surface roll out half the pastry (and then repeat with the other half) until 30 cm square.

2. Simply mince and combine the meat as for the Irish Breakfast Sausage (page 45). Divide into six equal portions and with your hands roll into sausage shapes the length of the pastry. Divide each pastry sheet into three sections and place the sausage meat in the middle of each piece of pastry.

3. Brush the edges of the pastry with a little water and fold the pastry over and press the edges together.

4. Cut each long sausage roll into four pieces and place on a greased baking sheet.

5. Glaze with beaten egg and bake for 25–30 minutes until golden brown.

Index of sausage recipes

* V = vegetarian

Eastern European sausages

Dishes using sausages, sauces and accompaniments